7 Steps to Better Written Policies and Procedures

Stephen B. Page

7 Steps to Better Written Policies and Procedures

Exercises and Suggestions to Improve your
Writing Skills for Policies and Procedures

Stephen Page
MBA, PMP, CSQE, CRM, CFC

Process Improvement Publishing
Westerville, Ohio USA

info@companymanuals.com

Address Printing and Ordering questions to:

Stephen Page
Process Improvement Publishing
PO BOX 1694
Westerville, Ohio 43086 USA
Email: info@companymanuals.com
FAX: 360-358-6991

ORDERING INFORMATION

Individual Sales: This book may be ordered through the author's web site (http://www.companymanuals.com/writingformat/index.htm) or through the above address.

Orders by U.S. Trade Bookstores and Wholesalers: Please contact the author at the above mailing address for pricing and shipping terms.

Library of Congress Cataloguing in Publication Data
Page, Stephen B. (1949 -)

>7 Steps to Better Written Policies and Procedures. Includes exercises, suggested answers, checklists, sample policies and procedures

>ISBN 1-929065-24-8

>Published: June 2001
>Reprinted: January 2002

Although I have extensively researched all sources to ensure the accuracy and completeness of the information contained in this book, I assume no responsibility for errors, inaccuracies, omissions, or other inconsistencies. Any slights against people or organizations are unintentional.

iv

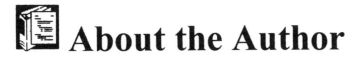# About the Author

Stephen B. Page is the author of six books, five of which focus on process improvement, business processes, policies, and procedures. Stephen holds a Masters of Business Administration (MBA) in Management from the University of California at Los Angeles (UCLA). He is certified as a project manager (PMP), software engineer (CSQE), records manager (CRM), and forms consultant (CFC).

His employment record contains an impressive list of multinational companies including Nationwide Insurance, Atos Origin, Compuware, Qwest Communications, Boeing Aircraft, Eastman Kodak, and Litton Industries. Stephen has more than 30 years experience in researching, writing, editing, publishing, communicating, training, measuring, and improving business processes, policies, procedures, and forms. He has written more than 250 company manuals in both printed and electronic formats and 6000 policies and procedures. He has designed 4000 forms and has set up manual and electronic form management systems. He has delivered policies and procedures in printed, network, web, CD-ROM, and video formats. He has first hand experience with the application of ISO Quality Standards, the Capability Maturity Model (CMM), Six Sigma, and the Malcolm Baldrige Award. Stephen has trained thousands of people in the art of writing effective policies and procedures.

Stephen has written many trade journal articles. His three most recent articles included two articles in 2001 on ISO 9000:2000 Quality Standards published in American Society of Quality's (ASQ's) Quality Progress Journal and in the QualityWorld magazine; and one article in 2000 published in ASQ's Quality Progress Journal on *"Research: The Key to Quality Policies and Procedures."* Stephen is a skilled presenter, facilitator, and team leader. He has participated on hundreds of team projects. He has presented seminars on the subject of printed and electronic policies and procedures, business processes, process improvement, and forms management.

Stephen has worked in various industries including consulting, manufacturing, telecommunications, financial banking, and retail. He has received dozens of awards for Total Quality Management (TQM) suggestions. In 2001, he received the "Malcolm Baldrige Award for Quality" from Atos Origin for his passion for quality, process improvement, and his high productivity.

Books by Stephen B. Page

Title	Publisher	©	URL (http://)
7 Steps to Better Written Policies and Procedures ISBN: 1929065-24-8	Process Improvement Publishing	2001	www.companymanuals.com/ writingformat/index.htm
Achieving 100% Compliance of Policies and Procedures ISBN: 1929065-49-3	Process Improvement Publishing	2000	www.companymanuals.com/ compliance/index.htm
Establishing a System of Policies and Procedures ISBN: 1929065-00-0	Process Improvement Publishing	1998	www.companymanuals.com
Putting Secrets for the Weekend Golfer (a putting process) ISBN: 0312-15197-7	St. Martin's Press	1997	Available through online booksellers
Business Policies and Procedures Handbook (Out of Print)	Prentice-Hall	1984	Replaced by "Establishing a System of Policies and Procedures"

How to Contact This Author

Stephen B. Page can be reached through the U.S. Mail, Email, FAX, and web site:

Stephen B. Page
PO BOX 1694
Westerville, Ohio 43086

Email: info@companymanuals.com
FAX: (360) 358-6991
URL: http://www.companymanuals.com/writingformat/index.htm

Table of Contents

Procedure	Ordering "Maintenance, Operating, Repair" (MRO) Supplies (Case Study)
Procedure	Organization Charts and Announcements
Policy	Bank Accounts

 # Introduction

The focus of this book is to show you how to use a structured writing method (called the WRITING FORMAT) for writing policies and procedures. Through exercises, suggested answers, and explanations of possible answers, you will learn how to transform ideas and concepts (generated from business processes) into structured, consistent, logical, and well written, sentences, and paragraphs (policies and procedures). Your policies and procedures will be easy-to-read, easy to apply, and comprehensive. Exercises, checklists, suggested answers, detailed explanations, and sample policies and procedures will ease you into this writing process. With this proven and tested WRITING FORMAT, you will have the opportunity to develop and improve your writing style. Your readers will thank you.

> My goal is for you to learn how to effectively use
> the Writing Format and to teach it to others.

For the purposes of this book, I am your teacher. I will give you enough information to make sound decisions when using the WRITING FORMAT and when teaching others how to use this writing method. I will give you ways you can succeed and become a better writer. I will give you exercises with "good" and "not so good" suggested answers to your responses. Each section of the WRITING FORMAT is methodically analyzed and explained to ensure you receive the best training possible. Two checklists are presented in Chapters 2 and 11 that will help you improve your editing abilities and help you write consistent and well laid-out policies and procedures. You will enhance your writing skills as a result of reading and doing the exercises in this book. With each chapter, you will gain valuable insight into ways that you can improve your writing style.

A key requirement of this book is that you must do the exercises to improve; and the more times you repeat the exercises, the better chance you will have in developing a writing style that matches or exceeds the suggested answers outlined in this book. Invaluable experience can be gained from these exercises. This book is a necessary addition for every person who owns one of my current books ("Establishing a System of Policies and Procedures" and "Achieving 100% Compliance of Policies and Procedures") because the WRITING FORMAT is the heart of any system of policies and procedures. The focus of any book on policies and procedures should be the WRITING FORMAT because without it, you would not have any way to record your thoughts.

This book emerged as the result of reader requests for real-life exercises using my recommended seven-step WRITING FORMAT (introduced in 1984) and sample written policies and procedures. This WRITING FORMAT has been successfully applied to thousands of companies in more than 25 countries. You will find the layout is easy to use once you have written several policies and procedures.

> *"I have often said that writing easy-to-read and comprehensive quality policies and procedures is an art that does not just happen. Sure, you can write the details of a policy or procedure, but to write quality documents that can be quickly understood and applied, is an art that comes only from experience, skill, and patience."*

While this book has been designed to accompany my two current books, any writer with a structured writing method (i.e., a writing format) for documenting policies and procedures, can use the concepts and principles contained in this book. The book has been set up so you can apply its principles, guidelines, and exercises to your daily work, team meetings, or training classes. Sample policies and procedures taken from companies where I have previously worked, have been included in Part 3.

This book does more than other books that try to teach how to write policies and procedures. Few authors cover the mechanics of transforming concepts into a structured outline of paragraphs, sentences, and words. Procedure authors often take the "writing" part of a policy or procedure system for granted. They fail to recognize that the WRITING FORMAT is the heart of a policies and procedures system.

The Writing Format is the heart of a policies and procedures system.

Writing policies and procedures is <u>not</u> free flowing writing like business letters or research papers. The writing skill for policies and procedures must be taught. Skills and techniques must be developed, trained, and mentored. Without a method of documenting policies and procedures, you could not achieve the consistency and standardization that management demands. Your system of policies and procedures is doomed to a slow death if writers are permitted to publish unstructured policies and procedures that change from one time to the next. The quality and effectiveness of your policies and procedures will have a major influence on your reputation as a procedure writer, and possibly, your continued career at your current place of work.

PLAN OF THE BOOK

This book is laid out in three parts:

- Part 1 – You are introduced to the writing format, the writing process, and an "Editing Checklist" for improving your writing style for policies and procedures.

- Part 2 – You are introduced to the case study that is the focus of the scenarios used for Chapters 4 to 10. Exercises, suggested answers, and explanations of these answers, are included for each of the seven sections of the WRITING FORMAT

- Part 3 – Three sample policies and procedures are presented for reference and comparison purposes.

While both printed and electronic formats exist, the focus of this book is on the WRITING FORMAT for printed policies and procedures. As is shown in my third book, "Establishing a System of Policies and Procedures," you can use the principles of the WRITING FORMAT for network and/or web formats. Many companies use a combination of printed, network, and web policies and procedures. Statistics show that few companies use network and/or web formats exclusively for company policy and procedure manuals. In each of the companies where I worked, we had both printed and electronic manuals (network and/or web). Providing different delivery formats (e.g., printed, network, web, CD, video, or other media yet identified or discovered) can be beneficial to readers who learn in different ways.

> The goal of this book is for you to improve your writing skills for policies and procedures and to write policies and procedures that are consistent, well written, and easily applied by your readers.

ACKNOWLEDGEMENTS

This book emerged from the experience I gained from writing my two current books on policies and procedures. Backed by multinational companies, I wrote these books while working in policy and procedure departments in large, and small companies in the manufacturing, banking, retail, telecommunications, and consulting industries. I have been using the same WRITING FORMAT for the past 30 years. From current book sales and reviews, it is apparent that my books have been well received. As a part of a series of books on policies and procedures, this new book will add value to the other two books because the WRITING FORMAT is the heart of any system of policies and procedures.

I owe many thanks to my readers who encouraged me to write this book through their emails, and kind letters. After reviewing sample policies and procedures from procedure writers that have adopted my WRITING FORMAT, I concluded that a book was needed to teach readers how to use and understand the mechanics of the WRITING FORMAT.

I thank the consulting team at the Columbus, Ohio branch of Atos Origin for encouraging me to write more books about my passion – helping others write effective policies and procedures.

I wish to thank Lisa Page, my daughter, for editing this book. She has a superb command of the language and I respect her comments. I also wish to thank Rhonda Myers, a current employee of American Electric Power in Columbus, Ohio, for taking time away from her busy personal life to carefully read this book. I consider her a peer in process improvement and I thought her comments would enhance this book.

I owe special thanks to my wife and family for allowing me to spend countless days, nights, and weekends to write, publish, and advertise this book. Without my wife's help and support with my book business, I could never have written this book.

Part 1

Introduction to the Writing Process

Chapter 1	Importance of a Writing Format
Chapter 2	The Writing Process

Chapter 1

Importance of a Writing Format

Objectives for this Chapter

- Establish importance of using a structured format for writing policies and procedures
- Demonstrate reasons for writing effective policies and procedures that readers can easily comprehend and apply
- Introduce a proven and tested WRITING FORMAT

Topics Include:

Purpose of a WRITING FORMAT
Plan of Action for Writing Policies and Procedures
WRITING FORMAT – The Layout
Frequently Asked Questions about the WRITING FORMAT

PURPOSE OF GOOD WRITING

Writing well is never easy. Most people, even professional writers, would agree that writing is a skill that does not come naturally. Writing requires great effort to combine creativity and attention to detail in a way that results in a product that people can read and understand with little effort. Whenever a writer puts pen to paper, or fingers to keyboard, as is more likely the case today, the potential exists for misunderstanding. Good writing means many things to different people. I believe the phrase, "I will know it when I see it," applies. If a writer has not defined the audience, purpose, or a focus, or if a document appears disorganized and hastily put together, the reader will be frustrated and confused. With good writing, your chance of reader comprehension and compliance increases.

You need to give the reader a roadmap and make it a smooth journey. The WRITING FORMAT is your roadmap; it will help the reader quickly understand the goals and objectives of a policy or procedure and lead him through the document from start to finish. Good writing is concise, clear, organized, and reader-specific. The purpose of any written document is to communicate thoughts or information. If readers cannot understand a document, communication is lost.

An editing checklist is introduced in Chapter 2, "The Writing Process," to provide you with some important questions to help you arrange your words, and sentences into well-written and logical paragraphs. A second checklist is introduced in Chapter 11, "Writing Format Checklist," to give you finality to your policy and procedure documents. With the writing process and these two checklists, you will achieve the goals of this book:

Goals for this Book	
1	Improve your writing skills for policies and procedures
2	Document policies and procedures that are structured, consistent, accurate, well written, and easy to understand and apply

Writing policies and procedures is an art form, and it takes years of experience, skill, and patience to become recognized by peers and management as being a "truly" good procedure writer.

IMPORTANCE OF "GOOD WRITING" FOR POLICIES AND PROCEDURES

The purpose of good writing to policies and procedures is to give the reader a document that is consistent, easy to read and apply, and that entices the reader to want to read and use the referenced policy or procedure in their daily work environment. Preparing well-written policy and procedure documents has advantages to you and your readers. For you, writing well makes you look good, get noticed, and even promoted. Second, good writing makes your manager, department, and company look good. Third, learning to write well is a skill you can add to your credentials. Fourth, good writing promotes consistency and standardization throughout your system of policies and procedures. Fifth, your readers will thank you for your efforts to write policies and procedures that are easy to read and apply.

For the reader, well-written policies and procedures often imply the documents are consistent, structured, and logical, and have good grammar, punctuation, and spelling. Second, well-written documents can often save reading time. With explicit section headings and well-constructed paragraphs and sentences, the reader can quickly scan a document and decide if a thorough reading warrants his time. Third, well-written documents suggest a qualified and skilled writer wrote them. If a writer has a good reputation for writing effective policies and procedures, the reader might look forward to the publication of new, or updated, policies and procedures.

PURPOSE OF A WRITING FORMAT

The Merriam-Webster's Dictionary defines format as, "a general plan of organization or arrangement." The term, "format," applies perfectly to writing policies and procedures because the structure, arrangement, and organization of process and procedural information are essential to understanding the facts presented. The task of standardizing the organization of policies and procedures falls into two steps: (1) grouping similar subjects and (2) linking those groups logically. The arrangement of these two steps is determined by a third element, a writing format.

> Think of a Writing Format as a way to present your policies and procedures in a structured and consistent format.

The WRITING FORMAT is the heart of any system of policies and procedures. This method of writing helps convert ideas and concepts into structured paragraphs, sentences, and words. The section headings are self-explanatory and arranged in a logical sequence made up of seven sections that is easy to follow. If these section headings were arranged differently from one time to the next, the reader would find it difficult to stay focused and understand the intent of the document. By using an unchanging sequence of section headings, the reader can stay focused as he reads through a policy or procedure. A busy reader can skim the section headings to find the sections of most interest, and relevancy. A well-written document makes its point quickly; efficiency is achieved with this WRITING FORMAT because a reader can understand the primary goals and objectives of a policy and procedure after reading just a few pages! You will appreciate the simplicity of the WRITING FORMAT when you become comfortable with its use and application. Writing policies and procedures can become simple and easy.

The hallmark of a successful format of writing lies in a standard writing structure, explicit section headings, and accurate content. The WRITING FORMAT solves a problem many business people face: <u>TIME</u>. In business, writing is a tool to get things done. Writers should assume that their readers are busy individuals who have little extra time to spend extracting information from a document.

A challenge often faced by procedure writers is that anyone with a word processor and a spell-checker thinks he can write policies and procedures. The manner in which policies and procedures are initiated varies from company to company. Some companies have staff policy and procedure departments while others have "would-be" procedure writers. And some companies have both a policies and procedures department and "would-be" procedure writers. Experienced procedure writers can always use a little extra help. For this reason, it can be a good idea to use the talents of "would-be" procedure writers. They can help with the initial research and writing process. Valuable "buy-in" can be gained by anyone who is assisting with the development of a new, or improved, process or procedure.

The WRITING FORMAT is an excellent tool because you can collect information sequentially or randomly – in both cases, when you have completed the seven sections, you will have a logical and coherent document. I have often used the term, "bucket," when referring to each section. The idea is to fill the buckets with information. This is an easy way for "would-be" procedure writers to understand their task: Simply ask them to fill in specific buckets and return the information to you. You will have gained in two ways: First, you will have extra research material that might be useful. Second, you will have gained allies from those "would-be" procedure writers who feel good about helping out. You will have the luxury of picking and choosing which material is the most relevant.

WRITING FORMAT – THE DETAILS

The WRITING FORMAT is written in an outline style with seven standard section headings. These headings provide information as well as visual breaks to reveal the structure of your text, thus making it easier to locate information, and follow the process flow. There are seven sections to the WRITING FORMAT, no more, no less:

1.0   Purpose
2.0   Revision History
3.0   Persons Affected
4.0   Policy
5.0   Definitions
6.0   Responsibilities
7.0   Procedures

Each section within the WRITING FORMAT is written in an outline format unless there is good reason to write it differently. The WRITING FORMAT is a part of a template used to visually display policies and procedures. The template contains three types of information: (1) identification information includes the title, policy or procedure identification number, effective date, revision date and number, page numbers, and approval signatures; (2) body of the policy or procedure, or the WRITING FORMAT; and (3) optional documentation that could be included at the end of policies and procedures.

The emphasis of this book is on two parts of the template, i.e., the WRITING FORMAT itself and the optional documentation. The development of the identification information is covered in my book entitled, "Establishing a System of Policies and Procedures."

The WRITING FORMAT is flexible and can be applied to any policy or procedure document. The only rigidity is in the number of sections. There are only seven sections, no more, no less. With few exceptions, every section is written in the outline format.

I had a personal experience where I was hired to replace a Policies and Procedures Manager in a large multinational company. This manager had been writing the company's policies and procedures in a paragraph style. The headings were inconsistent from document to document and his paragraphs were long and unstructured. He placed important points in the center of paragraphs. With this style of writing, he was inadvertently burying content in his paragraphs and unknowingly misleading management when they reviewed a document for approval.

When I was hired, I recommended that they use the seven-step WRITING FORMAT *that I had adopted from earlier companies.*

They asked that I show them a sample. I took a current procedure and converted it from the previous manager's writing style to my seven-step WRITING FORMAT *and did not change a single word: I simply restructured the paragraphs into an outline format for easier reading and comprehension. I gave the document to the Vice President of Finance to review. Shortly thereafter he stormed into my office and said "This is ridiculous, Stephen, you added information, I would never have signed this!" I calmly answered, "I did not change a single word. The current style of writing uses unstructured paragraphs that tend to hide content in long, wordy paragraphs and sentences. Let me show you (I laid the documents side by side). You will see that I did not add or delete a single word!" He was flabbergasted and concerned at what he had overlooked after realizing that I was correct. The company quickly converted to the new* WRITING FORMAT.

Poorly written policies and procedures do not support fast reading because major ideas are buried, headings are ambiguous or obscure to the reader, important details are hard to locate, and instructions are often nonexistent or difficult to find or understand. Consistent section headings from document to document save time because readers can quickly find the information they need and focus on content rather than format. More important, consistency coupled with informative section headings encourages the reader to believe that the document they are holding in their hand (or viewing on a computer screen) is a quality document and deserves their attention. This example illustrates the importance of finding a reputable WRITING FORMAT with logical section headings that guide you through the mechanics of transforming a business process into a policy or procedure document.

PLAN OF ACTION – WHERE THE <u>WRITING FORMAT</u> FITS

From my latest book, "Achieving 100% Compliance of Policies and Procedures," I am repeating a 40-step "Plan of Action" for transforming business processes into effective and well-written policies and procedures that can be quantified and measured. You will see that most of the 40 steps are inputs and outputs to the WRITING FORMAT. Details behind these steps can be found in my current books: "Establishing a System of Policies and Procedures" and "Achieving 100% Compliance of Policies and Procedures." The interesting truth is that the WRITING FORMAT is referenced in only one of the 40 steps. The other 39 steps are inputs, outputs, or provide administrative support to the WRITING FORMAT.

"PLAN OF ACTION" FOR POLICIES AND PROCEDURES

Management Action

1. Show commitment to the Policies and Procedures Department by including statements in their vision, mission, strategic goals, and objectives about writing effective business processes, policies and procedures, and for communicating, training, mentoring, measuring, and improving policies and procedures.

2. Assign a person or group to manage a policies and procedures function that will be accountable for the policies and procedures infrastructure from analysis to implementation and from compliance to improvement.

Procedure writer

3. Review the mission, vision, and strategic business goals of the organization. Compare these statements with the mission, vision, and strategic goals of the Policies and Procedures Department.

4. Identify processes, problems, issues, or concerns that need to be improved or documented.

5. Start identifying process owners, management sponsors, and primary user contacts.

6. Define the high level process, scope, mission, objective(s), and boundaries of the process.

7. Establish a cross-functional team to study the process for several alternate solutions. Establish a team charter, ground rules, and guidelines for the operation of the cross-functional team.

8. Select a team leader – the team leader is normally the procedure writer. If the team leader is not the procedure writer, the role of facilitator should be assigned to him so he can remain accountable for the business processes, policies, and procedures. The team leader can also serve as the facilitator.

9. Provide team training (e.g., problem-solving, listening skills, and interviewing skills, as well as the use of quality tools).

10.	Discuss a high level overview of the processes, issues, concerns, and challenges, and brainstorm with the team members.

11.	Challenge current assumptions and accepted business practices, processes, policies, and procedures.

12.	Define internal interfaces and responsibilities.

13.	Diagram the process flow (workflow) using a flow chart to depict the relationships of all the activities in the process.

14.	Identify problem areas, discuss and verify key causes, document and rank the causes using the Pareto analysis quality tool.

15.	Collect cost, time, and value data for future measurement purposes.

16.	Observe the business processes first-hand by "walking through" the various departments. Identify any new problems with the processes.

17.	Identify short-term improvements to the process.

18.	Concentrate on streamlining the processes, and resolving differences.

19.	Update the flow chart and write a summary of the tasks (i.e., task list) from the flow chart.

20.	Generate a list of possible solutions.

21.	Prioritize the solutions using the Pareto analysis quality tool, and select the most significant solution.

22.	Test the solution with the process owners, management sponsors, and primary users; identify any new issues and refine the solution. Redraw the flow chart and revise the task list.

23.	Transform the flow charts and task list into a draft policy or procedure using the standard WRITING FORMAT for policies and procedures.

24.	Obtain approvals of the draft policy or procedure from the cross-functional team, users, and other affected parties like customers or suppliers. Obtain approval from management and the individual designated as the final approval authority. Note the person making final signoff is often the person responsible for the overall compliance of the policy or procedure. As you will see in later chapters, the role of this person is listed as the first role in the *Responsibilities* section.

25. Establish communications, training, and review plans.

26. Publish the approved policy or procedure document.

27. Begin the communications campaign.

28. Conduct formal and informal training in accordance with the communication and training strategies.

29. Create a review and communication control plan.

30. Establish a compliance plan.

31. Conduct continuous improvement activities using quality tools like checklists, control charts, histograms, run charts, scatter diagrams, or the Pareto chart, to evaluate the effectiveness of the published policies and procedures.

32. Conduct system(s) audits.

33. Conduct improvement activities and cost benefit analyses.

34. Collect process data to verify that changes (from improvement activities) were effective and that they achieved the desired results.

35. Decide whether the changes were positive, or negative, and take the appropriate action(s).

36. Create file folders (physical and/or electronic) to maintain the collected data, flow charts, task lists, and policies and procedures for process improvement efforts.

37. Re-evaluate the compliance plan, change any compliance methods as appropriate, and make preparations to continue with the current compliance methods and/or start using the new list of compliance methods for the current business processes, policies, and procedures.

38. Communicate progress, in conjunction with the above steps, to process owners, sponsors, management, or users. Broadcast progress

about new or revised policies and procedures to the company through media described in the communications strategy.

39. Promote the activities of your policies and procedures group through the use of a "Policies and Procedures" newsletter or other available communications methods.

40. Add the policy or procedure to your previously published "Review Plan" to monitor events that might influence or support a current policy or procedure.

While the WRITING FORMAT may appear to play a small part in the scheme of things, policies and procedures could not exist without some form of structured method of writing. The significance of the WRITING FORMAT cannot be overemphasized. In absence of a writing format, the policies and procedures could not be formalized – the policies and procedures would remain unstructured thoughts in the heads of those making decisions. The whole purpose of the WRITING FORMAT is to give you a means by which to express your ideas in a logical, structured, meaningful, and documented manner.

RELEVANT STEPS THAT APPLY TO THE WRITING FORMAT

While just ONE step (Step 23) directly mentions the WRITING FORMAT, the WRITING FORMAT cannot be taken for granted! The selection and application of a WRITING FORMAT carries the same importance as any of the 40 steps!

Steps 1 to 9 are involved with administration and identification activities. Steps 10 to 22 are inputs to the WRITING FORMAT. Step 23 is the focus of the WRITING FORMAT. Steps 24 to 40 are outputs of the WRITING FORMAT.

> Step 23 states, *"Transfer process documentation and flow charts into a draft policy or procedure using a standard writing format for policies and procedures."*

WRITING FORMAT – A BRIEF DESCRIPTION OF ITS LAYOUT

The layout of the WRITING FORMAT always has seven sections. While the basic layout of the writing format has remained consistent for the past 30 years, I introduced one change with the release of my book, "Establishing a System of Policies and Procedures," in 1998. I added the *Revision History* to list changes and show an audit trail. In addition, there is only one writing format for both the policy and procedure document. The rationale for the use of a single writing format is addressed earlier in this chapter.

THE WRITING FORMAT

No	Section Heading
1.0	Purpose. Objectives for writing a policy or procedure.
2.0	Revision History. History of document changes.
3.0	Persons Affected. List of those persons or groups that might influence or support a specific policy or procedure.
4.0	Policy. General organizational attitude of an organization; a policy statement reflects the basic objectives, goals, vision, attitudes, or company culture.
5.0	Definitions. List of definitions of abbreviations, acronyms, words infrequently used, jargon, and technical terms. Optional documentation like forms, standards, diagrams, models, or reports are also defined and referenced.
6.0	Responsibilities. Short summary of the roles and responsibilities of the individuals that perform the actions of a policy or procedure.
7.0	Procedures. Explanations of the rules, regulations, methods, timing, place, and personnel responsible for accomplishing the policy as stated in Section 4.0 above. This section should follow the flow chart and task list created in Steps 13 and 19, respectively.
	Optional Documentation. Forms, diagrams, models, flow charts, or cumbersome text, are referenced either at the end of a policy or procedure or at an external location.

QUESTIONS AND ANSWERS ABOUT THE WRITING FORMAT

1. Do you use two writing formats, one for a policy and one for a procedure? The answer is "no." There is only one WRITING FORMAT, only the identification information and the content are different. Consistency and standardization are achieved when using the same section headings for both a policy or procedure document. The advantage of incorporating a policy section heading within a procedure document lies with the idea that two documents are incorporated into a single document. By incorporating a policy statement among procedural statements, the reader does not need to reference another source to complete his understanding of a policy or procedure! This method of writing makes it easier for writers and readers.

2. <u>My management still wants separate policies, where do I put them?</u> If you must have separate policies and procedures, do the following: Write a separate policy document using the seven-step writing format and either place the policy document in a separate policy manual or co-mingle the policy document with your procedure documents in a single manual. In this case, try color-coding the policy and procedure documents for visual separation purposes. In both cases, you should retain the *Policy* section heading within the seven-section WRITING FORMAT for consistency and standardization purposes. For further details on this practice, reference my book, "Establishing a System of Policies and Procedures," copyright 1998.

3. <u>Is it a good idea to have a separate policy and a separate procedures manual?</u> The answer is – it depends on your management. Some companies think it is a good idea to have separate policy and procedure manuals. Management thinks a policy manual is a good place to put all of the guidelines for their decisions. They believe there should be a separation of policy from procedural statements. In reality, these policy manuals are rarely referenced. Unless a standard or practice requires a policy manual, there is no logical reason to incur the extra expense.

4. <u>Why do you have a *Procedures* section within a Policy document?</u> Consistency is the key. Just like the retention of the *Policy* section within a procedures document, the retention of the *Procedures* section within a policy document maintains consistency of format. When writing a policy document, you can write, "Not Applicable," under the *Procedures* section heading if procedural statements do not apply. Refer to Part 3 for a sample policy that contains a *Procedures* section.

5. <u>Can I omit section headings?</u> The answer is "no." This is a mistake often made by inexperienced procedure writers. There are seven section headings within the WRITING FORMAT. These headings will always appear in the same sequence in a policy or procedure document, only the identification information and content will change.

REFERENCES

Bates, Jefferson D., <u>Writing with Precision, Sixth Edition</u>, Acropolis Books LTD, Washington, D.C., 1993.

Brown, Helen G., <u>The Writer's Rules</u>, William Morrow and Company, Inc., New York, New York 1998.

Cormier, Robin A., <u>Error-Free Writing</u>, Prentice Hall, Englewood Cliffs, New Jersey, 1995.

Kramer, Melinda G. and Leggett, Glenn, <u>The Writer's Rules</u>, C. David Mead, New York, New York, 1998.

Page, Stephen B., <u>Achieving 100% Compliance of Policies and Procedures</u>, BookMasters, Inc., Mansfield, Ohio, 2000.

Page, Stephen B., <u>Establishing a System of Policies and Procedures</u>, BookMasters, Inc., Mansfield, Ohio, 1998.

Sebranek, Patrick; Meyer, Verne; and Kemper, Dave, <u>Writer's Inc.</u>, Write Source, Wilmington, Massachusetts, 1996.

Slatkin, Elizabeth, <u>How to Write a Manual</u>, Ten Speed Press, Berkeley, California, 1991.

Sorenson, Sharon, <u>Webster's New World Student Writing Handbook</u>, Prentice Hall, New York, New York, 1992.

Venolia, Jan, <u>Rewrite Right!</u>, Ten Speed Press/Periwinkle Press, Berkeley, California, 1987.

Chapter 2

The Writing Process

Objectives for this Chapter

- Introduce the mechanics of writing and publishing policy and procedure documents
- Describe the value of using a writing process and an editing checklist for improving policy and procedure documents

Topics Include:

Writing Process
Editing Checklist
Writing Process – Five Steps
- Prewriting
- Preparing First Draft
- Editing Subsequent Drafts
- Coordinating Reviews and Approvals
- Publishing the Approved, Final Document

THE WRITING PROCESS

The process of transforming, or converting, business processes and supporting documentation into written policies and procedures is called the "The Writing Process." The process is a system of five steps for doing preparatory work; converting ideas into paragraphs, sentences, and words; editing the draft; coordinating reviews and approvals; and publishing the policy or procedure. These five steps of the writing process are:

1. Prewriting
2. Preparing the First Draft
3. Editing Subsequent Drafts
4. Coordinating Reviews and Approvals
5. Publishing the Approved, Final Document

Writing a policy or procedure document uses a method of business writing that is a combination of formal and informal writing. Unlike formal business correspondence, grammar and punctuation does not always follow all the rules. While the use of an editing checklist will enhance your policy and procedure writing skills, there will be instances where policy and procedure documents do not follow the rules. These exceptions will be explained in future chapters.

Word processors have blurred the distinction between writing and editing. The once sharply defined steps of writing, analyzing, and revising can now be integrated into a more smoothly flowing whole: You can revise as you write, and write as you revise. Even though the first four steps of the writing process overlap, each step should be treated as a distinct process when writing and publishing policies and procedures. The fifth step is likely to stand on its own. Once a policy or procedure is published, the writing process stops, and revision and improvement activities begin.

With policies and procedures, the term "research" is synonymous with "prewriting." For example, writing of the first draft, subsequent editing, and reviews can be blurred into a single step depending on how you like to write and coordinate policies and procedures. With most word processors, you are offered the opportunity to edit as you write. As reviews come in, you should edit and rewrite the draft policy or procedure to reflect the suggested changes. In addition, you should verify the content and suggested changes with the original contacts from the prewriting step. Publishing the approved, final document, is the only step of the writing process where an overlapping of steps is not likely to occur.

When a policy or procedure is published, the writing process stops and new processes begin. Following publication, the procedure writer has one primary goal: To ensure the readers comply with the guidelines of a policy or procedure. During this compliance phase, the procedure writer must focus on at least six areas: Communications, training, mentoring, compliance (metrics), auditing, and improvement activities. Many writers do not realize that writing policies and procedures is a process, an ongoing process, that cycles from writing to publication to training, from metrics to improvement, and to revisions of the policy or procedure (i.e., a new writing process). The writing process is continuous for the life of a policy or procedure. With my book, "Achieving 100% Compliance of Policies and Procedures," you can learn all the steps necessary to successfully accomplish the compliance phase (i.e., metrics to improvement to revisions to cost savings).

FIVE STEPS: THE WRITING PROCESS

1.   PREWRITING

The term "prewriting" refers to all the efforts to document and model a business process and to get ready to transform the information into a draft policy or procedure. Prewriting is about gathering the content for the topics selected for policy and procedure documents. Some authors call this step planning or research. I define prewriting as the research step. Research or prewriting is the step where your idea is conceived, your vision is formed, your team is selected, and research activities take place.

Regardless of what you name this step, you must do some kind of research, gather your thoughts and information, determine your purpose and goals, analyze the audience, and organize the material. Unless you are doing the research step yourself, you should conduct interviews and workshops, hold team meetings, take surveys, do questionnaires, document your findings, and do other necessary activities to collect information about a topic idea or problem. As long as you collect all the necessary information to write policy and procedure documents, how you collect the content is your choice.

You can use the WRITING FORMAT as a "writing aid" during the research step. As the WRITING FORMAT contains seven preset section headings, you can concentrate on each section as you gather your information. These section headings could become meeting topics or specific sections can be given to individuals or teams to fill in. While you can give out any section for research and completion, ultimately, you are accountable for the quality of the policies and procedures. Each section should be revisited and populated with the most relevant information collected during the prewriting or research step.

24

Index cards are another option for organizing your thoughts. You can label the cards with each of the relevant section headings as well as with potential topics of research. You can shuffle and rearrange these cards until you are satisfied with the process flow. The WRITING FORMAT helps you focus on the function of the outline, which is to help you arrange subjects for good communications.

2.   PREPARING THE FIRST DRAFT

Once you have completed the prewriting step, the writing process should be fairly simple. This step is especially easy if you use the "buckets" (section headings) concept of the WRITING FORMAT to fill in information as it is collected. While you might revisit the prewriting step throughout the writing process, you should only do so to verify information and check content references. With the prewriting step behind you, you are ready to begin your first draft. There are two parts to preparing the first draft: First, the structure or configuration of the WRITING FORMAT, and second, the process for writing the first draft. This second part will become clear once you complete the exercises on the WRITING FORMAT in Chapters 4 to 10.

"WRITING STRUCTURE" OF THE WRITING FORMAT

The WRITING FORMAT is written using an outline format. The formality of the outline intimidates some writers, but in reality, the outline is merely a list that shows the arrangement of details. The outline style for the WRITING FORMAT contains the following characteristics. Refer to Part 3 for sample policies and procedures that follow this exact format.

- Seven section headings, subheadings, and text make up the body of the WRITING FORMAT
- Numbers or Roman numerals are used for the numbering scheme of the outline format
- Section headings are left-justified and underlined (you could use normal text and all capitals or bold-faced type)
- Subheadings can be a heading and underlined or they can be full-length paragraphs or sentences (refer to the sample policies and procedures in Part 3 of this book)
- Each subheading of a heading, or another subheading, is represented by equal indentation
- The logic of development is arranged so that the summary parts of each subheading are equal to the topic of the section heading
- Paragraphs are structured such that each main idea, or subheading, represents a separate paragraph

An example of an outline format for the *Procedures* section follows:

7.0   Procedures (Section heading)

    7.1   Subheading or paragraph

        7.1.1   Subheading or paragraph
        7.1.2   Subheading or paragraph

            7.1.2.1 Subheading or paragraph
            7.1.2.2 Subheading or paragraph

    7.2   Subheading or paragraph

    Etc.

WRITING THE FIRST DRAFT

The WRITING FORMAT is flexible in its application. Some writers will insist on using note pads and writing down all the information first before entering any information into a word processor. While any method for capturing information is sufficient, you will need to enter the information into a word processor before giving it to reviewers. Try translating your notes directly into the WRITING FORMAT on your word processor to avoid excessive writing and rewriting of your notes. You should find this latter method more efficient because once you have completed filling in the preset section headings, you will have a rough draft of your new or revised policy or procedure.

The ease of making changes on a word processor frees you from concerns about how many drafts you will go through. Instead of starting the editing process in your head in order to minimize retyping, your fingers can quickly transform thoughts into words that you can see. Ideas are not lost while you struggle for the "perfect phrase." The very act of quickly putting the information in visible form helps sort the information. You can see that one idea is more important than another, that a good opening line is buried somewhere on the page, and so on. If you are stumped about a word or phrase, you can write a comment about it or bookmark it for later research.

There are two methods of populating the section headings of the WRITING FORMAT. First, you can add the information all at once. Somewhat like free writing, the principle is to capture as much information as possible. Keep writing until you have completed filling in the seven section headings. This approach is especially useful when you are facing a deadline. Second, you could complete the section headings in any sequence. You can give specific sections to individuals or teams to complete. This second approach is useful when the document is large and affects many functions or groups.

3.   EDITING SUBSEQUENT DRAFTS

Once you have a draft with which you are reasonably satisfied, your next step is to shift your focus and take a closer look at what you have written. During the second step, "Preparing the First Draft," you looked at the "big picture" and kept in mind your audience, purpose, and focus of the policy or procedure. You made sure everything made sense. You are now ready to start the editing process.

Some writers have trouble editing and revising because they become attached to their own words. They are reluctant to look for problems because finding them will only lead to more work, so they review their material quickly, with one eye closed. Other writers are never satisfied and continue to revise repeatedly until someone yanks them to their senses.

Editing is to improve something written – to make it easier to follow and more interesting to read. Basic editing primarily involves checking a document for organization, grammar, spelling, punctuation, stylistic consistency, and factual accuracy. While editing comes after the first draft, it can be a good idea to review the checklist ahead of time. You can eliminate many hours of future work using careful writing the first time. Knowing how to edit means knowing what makes good writing in the first place. Good writing comes from knowing how to revise and adjust words until they say what they are intended to say. Polished writing has a professional tone that reflects well on the general competence of the writer.

Editing of your first draft can be done directly on your word processor. Short documents that you have edited on the screen may survive with no further editing. You will find that if you have followed my advice about "filling in the buckets," (i.e., sections) you should have a completed document ready for review when you fill in your last bucket, especially if you paid attention to the grammar and spelling suggestions from your word processor.

While editing yourself is difficult, I do recommend that you do it the first time you read your own policies and procedures. Editing your own writing is easy with word processors because they have built-in grammar, punctuation, and spelling checkers. You can quickly change words by using the "search and replace" features. Insertions are easier, deletions are easier, moving sections around is easier, and working with clean, newly printed copies

27

makes it all worthwhile. If you have the luxury of having editors or technical writers in your company, you might be able to ask them to review your policies and procedures before sending them to reviewers and especially before sending them for final review and approval.

EDITING CHECKLIST

As you review what you have written, you may have an uneasy sense your document needs work. An "Editing Checklist" has been provided to help you understand possible problems with the organization of the paragraphs and sentences, grammar, punctuation, word usage, and spelling. Efficiency in editing comes not from a single all-purpose editing, but from several readings, each with a different focus. There are three levels of editing that should correspond with all, or part, of the review processes you have established for your policies and procedures. These three editing levels and their applicability are described in the following table:

NO	EDITING LEVEL	WHERE BEST APPLIED
1	Content – Section headings, logic, and factual accuracy	After writing the first draft (Step 2)
2	Language - Grammar, punctuation, and mechanics	During and after reviews are completed (Steps 3, 4)
3	Final Pass – Content and language	Prior to submission for final approval and review (Step 4)

The "Editing Checklist" contains the three editing levels. Copy the checklist and keep it as reference when you write new, or update existing, policies and procedures. Ideally, you review the checklist in advance to writing any policy or procedure document. At a minimum, keep the editing questions in mind when writing and incorporating changes to your policies and procedures.

Editing Checklist	
FIRST-LEVEL EDITING – CONTENT	
1	Verify the factual accuracy of your information.
2	Check for bias: Have you used slang words, inappropriate labels, or stereotypes? Have you given parallel treatment in matters of sex, race, age, and ability? Have you avoided ethnic slanted words?
3	Check for the correct audience: Is the writing directed to a specific reader, or a specific type of reader? Do you have the correct audience? Have you overlooked any potential audience? Does the writing style match what is known about that audience? Have you used words to fit the audience?

4	Check for logic: Are the ideas clear? Are the details adequate to describe the subject? Is the content easy to follow with clear, concise sentences? Is supporting material logical? Do you maintain credibility by avoiding hasty generalizations or faulty logic? Was a flow chart and task list used to write the first drafts? Do the paragraphs and sentences clearly follow the sequence of the flow chart steps and activities of the task list? Is the information coherent and straightforward? Are details supplied in proportion to importance? Does the *Purpose* section clearly present the reason for writing the policy or procedure? Does the *Policy* section follow the intent of the *Purpose* section? Does the *Procedures* section support the *Policy* section? Does the *Responsibilities* section support the flow of the *Procedures* section?
5	Check for clarity: Are any words or sentences ambiguous? Will readers always understand your use of vague pronoun references like what *it* and *they* and *this* refer to? Will readers be able to follow your train of thought? Have you used specific rather than vague words? Have you left a reader in doubt as to the meaning of critical words? Have you used the appropriate vocabulary for the audience?
6	Check for brevity or conciseness: Have you used too many words? Are their redundancies? Can you cut out words that do not add any additional meaning to a sentence?
7	Check for vocabulary usage: Have you used the right words to convey your meaning? Are singular and plural words used correctly? Have you used the active voice wherever possible? Does jargon create a verbal smokescreen? Have you used any jargon that has not been defined in the *Definitions* section? Do your words create the right kind of picture? Is the word choice appropriate for the audience? Are your words or phrases awkward, confusing, or misleading? Are your references confusing?
8	Check for paragraph usage: Does each paragraph have an overall point or purpose? Is each paragraph written in such a way so those sentences unfold to make your statements clear? Do you use an effective transition to move from your topic sentences to the first subtopics or supporting details? Does each paragraph have as its first sentence, a phrase that introduces the main topic? Does every paragraph have at least two sentences? Does each paragraph stand on its own and say something worthwhile?
9	Check for sentence usage: Are all your sentences complete thoughts? Are sentences 25 words or less? Are your sentences simple and clear? Are transitions adequate to move the reader from sentence to sentence and from paragraph to paragraph? Does every sentence bring unity to the paragraph and document?

SECOND-LEVEL EDITING – LANGUAGE	
1	Check for punctuation: Have you included accurate punctuation so that the meaning of sentences is clear? Do your punctuation marks help the reader grasp the meaning? Have you removed surplus punctuation? Have you omitted punctuation that would help the reader, e.g., did you remove a comma or semicolon that could have helped the reader better understand?
2	Check for grammar: Do subjects and verbs agree? Are pronouns in their correct case (e.g., *who* or *whom*, *I*, *me*, or *myself*)? Are verbs the correct tense? Is the tense and mood of verbs consistent? Do you have any fragmented or run-on sentences, other than those allowed by the WRITING FORMAT? Does your writing flow smoothly?
3	Check for mechanics: Have you maintained the structure of the WRITING FORMAT? Do you have a table of contents and does it accurately reflect the content of the policy or procedure draft? Have abbreviations been kept to a minimum? Are they correctly used? Is capitalization correct and consistent? Are words correctly spelled? Have you reviewed your use of numbers in text (should they be words or figures)? Are cross-references accurate?

THIRD-LEVEL EDITING – FINAL PASS	
1	Have you used the seven sections of the WRITING FORMAT for both a policy and procedure document?
2	Have all the reviews and comments been incorporated? Have you discussed any changes or omissions (from reviews) with those that submitted them?
3	Is your writing style the same throughout the document? Did you mix opening sentences?
4	Have you read your draft aloud to test it for sense and sound?
5	Have you performed one last reference and accuracy check?
6	Does the document reflect the current policies, procedures, and practices relevant to the writing of policies and procedures?

After you have completed the first two editing levels, you are ready to submit the policy or procedure draft for review. You will come back to the editing checklist for the third level of editing when you are ready to submit your final draft for review and approval.

4. OBTAINING REVIEWS AND APPROVALS

The review process can actually begin during the first several steps of the writing process and continue through the fourth step. Refer to the appropriate editing level when coordinating the review process. The number of reviews is your choice. The third level of editing should not take place until all reviews have been completed and all edits have been made. For details on user and management review processes, refer to my book entitled, "Establishing a System of Policies and Procedures."

5.   PUBLISHING THE APPROVED, FINAL DOCUMENT

Upon final approval, your next step is to publish the document. Methods and guidance for publishing your document are contained in my two current books. Once you have published the policy or procedure document, your job is just beginning. The writing process is a continuous process that starts with a new document and is continuously revised until the document is removed from the system of policies and procedures. At this time, you should begin developing communications, mentoring, training, metrics, auditing, and improvement plans.

REFERENCES

Bates, Jefferson D., Writing with Precision, Sixth Edition, Acropolis Books LTD, Washington, D.C., 1993.

Brown, Helen G., The Writer's Rules, William Morrow and Company, Inc., New York, New York 1998.

Dobrian, Joseph, Business Writing Skills, AMACOM, New York, New York, 1998.

Kramer, Melinda G. and Leggett, Glenn, The Writer's Rules, C. David Mead, New York, New York, 1998.

Page, Stephen B., Achieving 100% Compliance of Policies and Procedures, BookMasters, Inc., Mansfield, Ohio, 2000.

Page, Stephen B., Establishing a System of Policies and Procedures, BookMasters, Inc., Mansfield, Ohio, 1998.

Ross-Larson, Bruce, Edit Yourself, W.W. Norton & Company, New York, New York, 1996.

Ross-Larson, Bruce, Powerful Paragraphs, W.W. Norton & Company, New York, New York, 1999.

Ross-Larson, Bruce, <u>Stunning Sentences</u>, W.W. Norton & Company, New York, New York, 1999.

Sebranek, Patrick; Meyer, Verne; and Kemper, Dave, <u>Writer's Inc.</u>, Write Source, Wilmington, Massachusetts, 1996.

Slatkin, Elizabeth, <u>How to Write a Manual</u>, Ten Speed Press, Berkeley, California, 1991.

Sorenson, Sharon, <u>Webster's New World Student Writing Handbook</u>, Prentice Hall, New York, New York, 1992.

Venolia, Jan, <u>Rewrite Right!</u> Ten Speed Press/Periwinkle Press, Berkeley, California, 1987

Part 2

Case Study, Exercises, and Suggested Answers

Chapter 3	Case Study and Scenario
Chapter 4	1.0 <u>Purpose</u>, First Section
Chapter 5	2.0 <u>Revision History</u>, Second Section
Chapter 6	3.0 <u>Persons Affected</u>, Third Section
Chapter 7	4.0 <u>Policy</u>, Fourth Section
Chapter 8	5.0 <u>Definitions</u>, Fifth Section
Chapter 9	6.0 <u>Responsibilities</u>, Sixth Section
Chapter 10	7.0 <u>Procedures</u>, Seventh Section
Chapter 11	Writing Format Checklist

Chapter 3

Case Study and Scenario

Objectives for this Chapter

- Set the stage for the case study and scenarios for the exercises in Chapters 4 to 10
- Review assumptions that might influence your interpretation of the exercises and suggested answers

Topics Include:

Purpose of Scenario
Assumptions for Chapters 4 to 10
Case Study – The Scenario
"Purchasing Process" for the Case Study
- Background of Purchasing Process
- First Reference – Flow Chart
- Second Reference – Task List
Transforming the Purchasing Process into a Procedure
Purpose and Application of Exercises in Chapters 4 to 10

PURPOSE OF CASE STUDY AND SCENARIO

The focus of this book is to show you how to use the WRITING FORMAT to achieve consistent, logical, and well-written policies and procedures. A case study is borrowed from my current book, "Achieving 100% Compliance of Policies and Procedures," to provide scenarios for the exercises contained in Chapters 4 through 10. Pertinent sections will be selected for the development of scenarios for each section of the WRITING FORMAT. The written procedure for the case study is referenced in Part 3 of this book.

ASSUMPTIONS TO CONSIDER FOR CHAPTERS 4 through 10

There are specific assumptions that need to be addressed before the case study and background information are introduced. Understanding these assumptions up front will help you when reading these chapters and doing the exercises.

- I have selected the scenario I used to produce the case study referenced in my latest book, "Achieving 100% Compliance of Policies and Procedures." I will reference the flow chart as well as the task list. Both references are important information to consider when writing your policy or procedure documents. While there are other references collected during the prewriting step, these are the two references I use for the scenarios.

- The format of the title, identification number, dates, revision number, and approval fields on the WRITING FORMAT template are for example purposes only.

- The WRITING FORMAT contains seven steps. The numbering scheme begins with 1.0 and ends with 7.0. Each subsequent subheading will be indented five or more spaces.

- Each section heading will be underlined and left justified.

- The issue of using a separate policy manual, or housing policies and procedures in a single company manual, is being ignored for the purposes of these exercises.

- Each section within the WRITING FORMAT will be addressed independent of the type of document, i.e., the subtle differences between a policy and procedure document will be ignored.

- When the *Procedures* section (i.e., seventh section heading) is addressed, the document type used for the exercises will be a procedure document because a policy document traditionally does not require any information to be entered into this seventh heading.

- Optional documentation like diagrams or models will be discussed in Chapter 8, "5.0 <u>Definitions.</u>" Actual forms will not be shown in the exercises or the sample policies and procedures referenced in Part 3.

CASE STUDY – THE SCENARIO

During the normal course of a day, the procedure writer often encounters situations that warrant his attention. A typical day goes like this:

> You have been spending time in the company's Purchasing Department and you have observed that the process for the purchase of office supplies and tools seems awkward, inconsistent, and repetitious, and employees are making numerous mistakes. The Purchasing Department has informed you that the purchase requisition form is being used inconsistently: Company checks, personal checks, and cash are being used to purchase supply items. The Purchasing Department is alarmed because unauthorized and inexperienced employees are buying directly from suppliers and placing the company at a liability risk.
>
> In addition, the Accounting Department is requesting the Purchasing Department approve the invoices of these unauthorized orders. The Purchasing Department is reluctant to sign off an invoice when the order placement did not go through them. The Purchasing Department has asked you to look into the whole process of purchasing office supplies and tools commonly known as MRO supplies.
>
> You have received approval from your manager to review the Purchasing Process and write the procedure. You can now make preparations to begin the research or prewriting step.

While the results of your research and meetings should yield many useful documents and diagrams, I have included a "Flow Chart" of the major steps in the process and a "Task List" that describes the steps in the flow chart. With this knowledge, the procedure writer can begin writing the first draft by populating the sections of the WRITING FORMAT.

"PURCHASING PROCESS" CASE STUDY AND BACKGROUND

The case study documents a "Purchasing Process." This case study was selected because many readers should be able to identify with the process of filling out a form to purchase items. In a general sense, "purchasing" describes a buying process. In a broader context, "purchasing" involves determining the need, selecting a supplier, arriving at an appropriate price, writing terms and conditions, issuing an order, following up to ensure delivery and inspection, and paying an invoice.

A purchasing process typically covers the purchase of all items from office supplies to major capital investments. The purchasing process includes the sub-processes, policies, procedures, and forms for acquiring items and services for an organization. The magnitude and make up of the purchasing process depends on the type and size of an organization, company policies and procedures, management attitudes, company culture, and computer technology.

In this case study, I narrowed the focus of the purchasing process to the purchase of supply and office-type items that are not for resale or production purposes. These types of items are referred to as "MRO" items, or "Maintenance, Repair, and Operating" supply items. In a manufacturing environment, MRO orders can account for 80% of the volume of paperwork while administrative time accounts for the remaining 20%. A detailed flow chart is illustrated for the *Purchasing Process* on the following page. A 16-step task list is derived from the flow chart. The flow chart and task list will be used as the basis of the scenarios for the exercises in Chapters 4 to 10.

BACKGROUND OF "PURCHASING PROCESS"

The case study is based on the purchasing system in a printer manufacturing company in Woodland Hills, California. There are 3600 employees worldwide. The corporate Purchasing Department is located in Woodland Hills, California and they have 40 employees. There are ten Buyers, two of which are MRO Buyers responsible for small tools, maintenance items, and office supplies. There are three Purchasing Managers responsible for different commodities, three Purchasing Agents that support the Managers, two Purchasing Assistants for the three Managers, and one Purchasing Supervisor that supervises the administrative functions of the department. A Purchasing Director oversees the Purchasing Department. Expediters, purchasing analysts, and administrative support make up the rest of the purchasing staff. There are 15 Purchasing Departments outside of North America; each department follows its own set of rules.

There are three ways to request purchases:

1. A standard "Purchase Requisition" (PR) form (herein referred to as a "purchase requisition") is used for purchases made on a one-time basis. While purchase requisitions are used for purchases of less than $5,000.00, the purchase requisition is typically used for MRO supply items that are not-for-resale, not for production, and cost less than $500.00.

2. A "Traveling Requisition" is used for items purchased on a regular basis (like tools or low-cost items used for production).

3. A computerized Bill of Material (BOM) and Material Requirements Planning (MRP) Schedule is used for ordering production items.

FIRST REFERENCE – FLOW CHART

The two major outputs of the research or prewriting step are the flow chart and task list. These two reference documents are the primary sources of information for the scenarios and exercises in Chapters 4 to 10. The flow chart of the purchase requisition process is illustrated below:

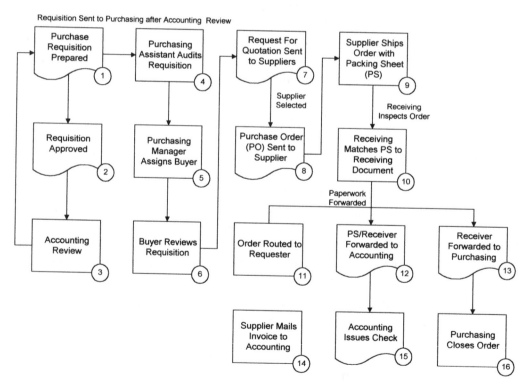

SECOND REFERENCE – TASK LIST

The "Task List" is your second major reference document. For your exercises in Chapters 4 through 10, you should copy the flow chart and the task list for easy reference. Each step within the task list matches a step in the flow chart. Once the task list is completed, it becomes a relatively easy process to transform these activities into the *Responsibilities* and the *Procedures* sections of the WRITING FORMAT.

The 16-step "Task List" is as follows:

1   Purchasing Requisition (PR) Prepared. The employee prepares a three-part PR for specific MRO supply items and sends the purchase requisition to his supervisor or manager for approval.

2   Purchasing Requisition Approval. The employee's supervisor (or manager) makes the decision to approve or disapprove the PR. If the value of the PR exceeds $250.00 and is less than $500.00, a second signature is needed. The supervisor sends the purchase requisition to his manager for approval, as appropriate.

3   Accounting Review. The employee's supervisor sends the approved PR to the accounting department for budget, charge (or account) number, and signature authorization review.

The accounting department returns the purchase requisition to the employee. The employee removes the last copy and sends the purchase requisition (original and copy) to the purchasing department for processing

4   Purchasing Assistant Audits the Purchasing Requisition. The purchasing assistant is the first point of contact in the purchasing department to review purchase requisitions. This person reviews the purchase requisitions to ensure they are completed in accordance with the current purchasing processes and procedures. The purchasing assistant initials the purchase requisition if it passes the review process and forwards it to a purchasing manager. Otherwise, the purchasing assistant contacts the employee to discuss noncompliance issues.

5   Purchasing Manager Assigns Buyer. The purchasing manager reviews the purchase requisition, notes the appropriate buyer

on the form, initials the form next to the initials of the purchasing assistant, and forwards the purchase requisition to the buyer.

6   Buyer Reviews Purchase Requisition. The buyer reviews the purchase requisition and determines the course of action for selecting a supplier, by viewing published lists, blanket order contracts, purchase history, and new suppliers.

7   Request for Quotation (RFQ) Sent to Suppliers. The buyer sends a three-part RFQ form to at least three suppliers to obtain competitive bids. The buyer selects one supplier based on the returned bids.

8   Purchase Order (PO) Sent to Supplier. The buyer prepares a five-part PO form and separates it by mailing two copies to the selected supplier, the third copy to the purchasing department, the fourth copy to the accounting department, and the fifth copy to the receiving department.

The receiving department reproduces a "Receiver Set" based on the "PO" copy, by photocopying, and using a four-part, pre-collated, set of colored paper (herein referred to as the "receiver.")

9   Supplier Ships Order with Packing Sheet (PS). The supplier fills the order in accordance with the terms and conditions of the PO; the supplier packages the order, and ships the order to the employee's shipping department, along with a two-part packing sheet.

10   Receiving Matches PS to Receiver. The receiving department counts the quantity of the received order and matches the order quantity to both the PS and receiver.

Depending on the type and dollar value of the item(s) ordered, an inspection department might inspect the order before it is forwarded to the employee.

11   Order Routed to Employee of Items. The receiving department completes the receiver and forwards the received items to the employee.

12   PS/Receiver Forwarded to the Accounting Department. The receiving department forwards copies of both the packing

sheet and the receiver document to the accounting department for payment.

13   Receiver Forwarded to the Purchasing Department. The receiving department forwards a copy of the receiver to the purchasing department for follow up on the order and to close the order when it is confirmed that the order has been received, inspected, and paid.

14   Supplier Mails Invoice to the Accounting Department. The supplier mails the invoice to the organization's accounting department for payment.

15   The Accounting Department Issues Check. The accounting department matches the packing sheet with the receiver and/or PO and keeps the two documents together until the invoice is matched. A check is created and mailed (printed check or electronic funds transfer) to the supplier.

16   Purchasing Department Closes the Order. The purchasing department closes the order and files it for reference purposes after the buyer receives notification that the items have been received.

TRANSFORMING THE PURCHASING PROCESS INTO WORDS

With these two references (flow chart and task list) and any other information collected, you are ready to start writing your procedure. Before you actually write the procedure, there are two additional steps:

- Create, or select, a template format for the WRITING FORMAT that includes fields for the identification information of a policy or procedure. The method used in the examples is one of many possibilities. You can design a template for your word processor, design a screen format on a network, design a web form, or design forms that can be printed. The choice is yours.

- Decide on a title for the policy or procedure document. As this procedure is about purchasing MRO items, the title of the procedure could be "Purchasing System Maintenance, Repair, and Operation (MRO) Supplies" or "Ordering MRO Supplies." The latter title is not acceptable because the abbreviation, "MRO," has yet to be defined. While it is tempting to use this shorter title, it does not follow the rules of grammar.

PURPOSE OF EXERCISES IN CHAPTERS 4 to 10

Exercises are drills that should be completed for training and improvement of writing skills for policies and procedures. Reading the exercises will do nothing for you: You must do the exercises! And you must repeat the exercises! Without actual practice, you will not get the benefits intended from this book. The scenario for each exercise is based on the flow chart and task list in this chapter. The information provided for the exercises will be the minimum required for you to complete your answers. Write or key your responses to exercises on a notepad or in your word processor. The latter method is preferred because you can easily edit your answers and save them for reference purposes. When you have completed the exercises, you will be ready to write any policy or procedure. With experience, patience, and skill, you will start writing better policies and procedures.

NOTE: The suggested answers in the following chapters will not necessarily be reflected in the procedure (case study) referenced in Part 3 of this book.

REFERENCES

Dobrian, Joseph, Business Writing Skills, AMACOM, New York, New York, 1998.

Harding, Michael and Mary Lu, Purchasing, Barrons, Hauppage, New York, 1991.

Page, Stephen B., Achieving 100% Compliance of Policies and Procedures, BookMasters, Inc., Mansfield, Ohio, 2000.

Page, Stephen B., Establishing a System of Policies and Procedures, BookMasters, Inc., Mansfield, Ohio, 1998.

Ross-Larson, Bruce, Edit Yourself, W.W. Norton & Company, New York, New York, 1996.

Venolia, Jan, Rewrite Right!, Ten Speed Press/Periwinkle Press, Berkeley, California, 1987

Chapter 4

1.0 <u>Purpose</u>
First Section, Writing Format

Objectives for this Chapter

- Describe the purpose of this first section and its importance to the WRITING FORMAT
- Provide a complete analysis of the "do's" and "don'ts" of the *Purpose* section
- Provide questions and suggested answers to your responses to the *Purpose* exercises

Topics Include:

Sample Template and WRITING FORMAT
Purpose of Section 1: <u>Purpose</u>
Format of <u>Purpose</u> Section
Common Mistakes
Scenario of <u>Purpose</u> Section
What to Look For
<u>Purpose</u> Exercise
Good Answers
"Not So Good" Answers
Checking your Work
Summary
References

A TEMPLATE AND WRITING FORMAT

	Document No.	
	Effective Date	
	Revision Date	
TITLE OF POLICY or PROCEDURE	Revision No.	
	Page No.	
	Approval:	

1.0   Purpose

Describes objective(s) for writing a policy or procedure.

2.0   Revision History

Shows list of document changes to this document.

3.0   Persons Affected

Identifies the users of this document.

4.0   Policy

Describes the general organizational attitude of the company.

5.0   Definitions

Defines abbreviations, acronyms, forms, words infrequently used and technical terms.

6.0   Responsibilities

Summarizes the roles and responsibilities of all individuals involved with this document.

7.0   Procedures

Defines and outlines the rules, regulations, methods, timing, place, and personnel responsible for accomplishing the policy as stated in the *Policy* section above.

PURPOSE OF SECTION 1: <u>PURPOSE</u>

This is the first section heading of the WRITING FORMAT. The *Purpose* section contains an introductory paragraph that explains the objective(s) and reasons for writing a policy or procedure in the first place. The *Purpose* paragraph should be comprehensive and concise in its meaning. From the title and the introductory paragraph, the reader should have a clear sense of what to expect in the rest of a policy or procedure document.

FORMAT OF *<u>PURPOSE</u>* SECTION

The *Purpose* section is generally limited to one paragraph made up of two or three sentences in addition to an opening sentence. The outline format, including subheadings and bullets, is not acceptable. When writing *Purpose* statements, you should consider an opening phrase that you can use from policy to policy and from procedure to procedure.

A format for a good opening sentence follows: "This [insert 'policy' or 'procedure'] establishes guidelines for..." A subdivided opening sentence is also acceptable. For example, "This procedure establishes guidelines for: (1) creating organization charts and (2) publishing announcements." A single sentence purpose is acceptable in some circumstances.

IS THE *<u>PURPOSE</u>* SECTION REQUIRED OR OPTIONAL?

The *Purpose* section is required for policies and procedures. The format of the first sentence of every *Purpose* section should be the same.

COMMON MISTAKES

The common mistakes for the *Purpose* section include:

- Omitting the *Purpose* section heading
- Failing to write a *Purpose* statement that introduces the main topic that later supports the *Policy* statement
- Writing lengthy *Purpose* paragraphs
- Using an outline format, subheadings, or bullets
- Using fragmented sentences
- Using abbreviations, acronyms, or other technical terms not yet defined or readily recognized by the audience
- Failing to use a consistent opening phrase from policy to policy or from procedure to procedure

SCENARIO OF THE PURPOSE SECTION

The scenario for the *Purpose* section contains information that was collected during the research or prewriting step. The business processes, diagrams, meeting results, or other documents, become the input to this section. The information can also be used for the *Policy*, *Responsibilities*, and *Procedures* sections. In this scenario, you know the following:

- Employees purchase supply items in multiple ways including purchase requisition, company or personal check, credit card, or cash
- Employees are inadvertently putting the company at risk by going around the professionals in the purchasing department who have been approved by the company to commit funds to suppliers for duly authorized orders and contracts
- Discovery that maintenance, repair, operating (MRO), and office supplies are not-for-resale, not used in production, and cost less than $500.00
- The goal of the purchasing department is to become a single point of procurement activities for all employee purchase requests

WHAT TO LOOK FOR

Look for information that will lead you to an introductory statement. Look for words and phrases that tell the story about the subject or solution to the original problem statement. If you just start writing the opening phrase, "The [insert policy or procedure] establishes guidelines for..." the rest of the sentence should flow naturally as you recall the information collected during the prewriting or research step.

PURPOSE EXERCISE

Write two sentences that describe the intention of a procedure for employees who wish to purchase maintenance, repair, and operating (MRO) supply items like small tools or office supplies. Compare your responses with the suggested answers and explanations in the next few pages. Record your answers on a notepad or word processor. Save your work.

GOOD ANSWER

1.0   Purpose

This procedure establishes guidelines for the business process by which employees can request the purchase of maintenance, repair, and operating (MRO) supplies directly from the purchasing department. The process begins with a purchase requisition being completed; the process ends with the payment of an invoice.

Explanation of Answer:

The intention of this statement is made clear by using a two-sentence purpose statement. The opening phrase is clear – notice how the sentence is worded almost like a definition. This is an excellent way to begin policy and procedure documents. The opening phrase can be reused for future procedures. In the second sentence, a starting and ending point is indicated. With this distinct 'Purpose' statement, the reader can expect the procedure to unfold with details that explain how and when a purchase requisition should be used. Both sentences are quantifiable and measurable.

"NOT SO GOOD" ANSWERS

Answer 1:

1.0   Purpose

This procedure establishes guidelines for employees to request the Purchasing Department to purchase items.

Explanation of Answer:

In this case, a single sentence is not enough. Had the sentence been more descriptive, it could have been acceptable. Several details are missing. The reader is not certain how the employee requests items from the purchasing department. The word, purchase requisition, is not even used. Also, by using the word, 'request,' rather than 'purchase requisition,' the process by which supply items are requested could be misinterpreted. The purchasing department wants a purchase requisition to be processed by the employee; they are not looking for telephone calls, emails, faxes, or walk-ins. When writing 'Purpose' statements, try to make some kind of reference to the title of the policy or procedure.

Answer 2:

1.0   Purpose

It is the purpose of this document to provide guidelines for the Purchasing Department to accept PR's from employees. The process starts with the initiation of a purchase requisition and ends with the completion of a PO and invoice payment by AP.

Explanation of Answer:

The statements in Answer 2 are stronger than in Answer 1, but the statement is still vague. The opening sentence is in the passive voice and the sentence starts with "it," a poor choice in any business document. The use of the word 'document' leaves the reader confused about the document type – is it a policy or a procedure? The abbreviations, PR, PO, and AP are not acceptable because they have yet to be defined. If you had defined any of these terms in the title, you could have used the appropriate abbreviation.

CHECKING YOUR WORK

Verify that your *Purpose* statement does not violate any of the "Common Mistakes." Check the content of your introductory paragraph with the scenario section.

SUMMARY

The *Purpose* statement is the first section of the WRITING FORMAT. This section serves the purpose of introducing the main focus of the policy or procedure. The paragraph is the preferred format of the *Purpose*. The reader should have a clear sense of how the document will unfold from these two or three sentences.

REFERENCES

Dobrian, Joseph, Business Writing Skills, AMACOM, New York, New York, 1998.

Page, Stephen B., Achieving 100% Compliance of Policies and Procedures, BookMasters, Inc., Mansfield, Ohio, 2000.

Page, Stephen B., Establishing a System of Policies and Procedures, BookMasters, Inc., Mansfield, Ohio, 1998.

Chapter 5

2.0 <u>Revision History</u>
Second Section, Writing Format

Objectives for this Chapter

- Describe the purpose of this second section and its importance to the WRITING FORMAT
- Provide a complete analysis of the "do's" and "don'ts" of the *Revision History* section
- Provide questions and suggested answers to your responses to the *Revision History* exercises

Topics Include:

Sample Template and WRITING FORMAT
Purpose of Section 2: <u>Revision History</u>
Format of <u>Revision History</u> Section
Common Mistakes
Scenario of <u>Revision History</u> Section
What to Look For
<u>Revision History</u> Exercise
Good Answers
"Not So Good" Answers
Checking your Work
Summary
References

A TEMPLATE AND WRITING FORMAT

	Document No.	
	Effective Date	
TITLE OF POLICY or PROCEDURE	Revision Date	
	Revision No.	
	Page No.	
	Approval:	

1.0   Purpose

Describes objective(s) for writing a policy or procedure.

2.0   Revision History

Shows list of document changes to this document.

3.0   Persons Affected

Identifies the users of this document.

4.0   Policy

Describes the general organizational attitude of the company.

5.0   Definitions

Defines abbreviations, acronyms, forms, words infrequently used and technical terms.

6.0   Responsibilities

Summarizes the roles and responsibilities of all individuals involved with this document.

7.0   Procedures

Defines and outlines the rules, regulations, methods, timing, place, and personnel responsible for accomplishing the policy as stated in the *Policy* section above.

PURPOSE OF SECTION 2: REVISION HISTORY

This is the second section heading of the WRITING FORMAT. The *Revision History* section describes changes, or updates, to a policy or procedure. A history of changes serves as a reference for the reader to understand any changes made to a policy or procedure. In addition, a list of document changes can be useful for metrics and measurements, and for audit purposes.

FORMAT OF REVISION HISTORY SECTION

The format of the *Revision History* is your choice. My preference is a four-column table. Though you could present the same information without the table borders. For each change, the date, revision number, and references are included. The date and revision number are recorded in this table as well as in the identification fields of the template used for policies and procedures.

Date	Rev. No.	Change	Reference Section(s)

- Date column: Date of new policy or procedure and subsequent changes. The first entry is the "effective date" of the document.
- Revision Number column: The first number is 1.0 and represents a new document. For each change, the number increments upward.
- Change column: This column can be written with the reason for change in a fragmented sentence. For a new document, the word, "New [insert 'Policy' or 'Procedure']," is entered into this column.
- Reference Sections column: Section references for each change. Use the "search" feature of your word processor to locate references.

IS THE REVISION HISTORY SECTION REQUIRED OR OPTIONAL?

The *Revision History* section is required for policies and procedures. This section is used for new documents as well as for all subsequent changes. The new document is your baseline for improvement and audit purposes.

COMMON MISTAKES

The common mistakes for the *Revision History* section include:

- Omitting the *Revision History* section for new documents and for subsequent changes to the original document

- Failing to enter information for a "New" document in the first row
- Failing to complete the *Revision History* section for changes
- Failing to increase revision numbers for changes
- Writing change descriptions which are too short to be meaningful
- Omitting small changes like a title change or spelling error
- Omitting a reference to a section
- Failing to find correct references

SCENARIO OF THE <u>REVISION HISTORY</u> SECTION

The scenario for the *Revision History* section is derived from two sources: First, if a policy or procedure is being published for the first time, then the *Revision History* table is used to record the identification information for this new document. Second, a change has to occur in a document before a revised policy or procedure is written. Changes to policies and procedures come from three sources: (1) suggestions from users of a policy or procedure, (2) observations by the procedure writers, and (3) as the result of metrics and improvement plans. In this section, you know the following:

- This procedure for MRO supply items is a "new" procedure
- The Purchasing Director has been promoted to Purchasing Department Executive
- The Purchasing Assistant title has been changed to Purchasing Administrator
- The Purchasing Department has added a debit card as an alternative to using the purchase requisition for purchase requests

WHAT TO LOOK FOR

Look for any change, no matter how minor. Any time you make a change to a specific policy or procedure, an entry should be added to the *Revision History* table. Use the "search" or "find" features of your word processor for locating all references to a proposed change. Record each section heading or subheading number (e.g., 4.2, 5.2, or 6.2.2.1), in the "Reference Section(s)" column.

REVISION HISTORY EXERCISE

Write three revision lines using the following information: (1) notice of a new procedure being drafted; (2) addition of a debit card; and (3) title changes for the Purchasing Director and Purchasing Assistant. Recreate the sample table from this chapter and do the exercises. Record your answers on a notepad or word processor. Save your work.

GOOD ANSWER

2.0 <u>Revision History</u>

Date	Rev. No.	Change	Reference Section(s)
06/04/2001	1.0	New procedure drafted	Not Applicable
08/15/2001	1.1	Debit card has been added as an alternative to the purchase requisition form	4.2, 5.2, 6.2, 7.2.3
10/05/2001	1.2	Purchasing Director title has been changed to Purchasing Department Executive due to a promotion	6.1, 7.1
		Purchasing Assistant title has been changed to Purchasing Administrator	6.3, 7.2.1

<u>Explanation of Answer</u>:

The above example is how a typical 'Revision History' table should be displayed in a policy or procedure document. Notice how the table is aligned under the section heading.

- *In row one, revision '1.0,' a new procedure is being introduced and the reference section has been marked as "Not Applicable." The effective date has been recorded. The phrase in the 'Change' column is a fragmented sentence: This usage is acceptable for the 'Revision History' section.*

- *In row two, revision '1.1,' a change to the procedure is introduced on 06/04/2001. Additional details of the change should be detailed in the 'Policy' and 'Procedures' sections.*

- *In rows three and four, revision '1.2,' two title changes have been entered. Notice how the revision numbers increment from 1.0 to 1.1 to 1.2. The titles of the Purchasing Director and the Purchasing Assistant have changed; you will want to find all instances of these titles by doing a search of your document.*

A fourth row was added to make a distinction that there were two title changes. Had both titles been placed on one row, there would be no way to separate the section references for each title.

"NOT SO GOOD" ANSWER

2.0   Revision History

Date	Rev. No.	Change	Reference Section(s)
06/04/2001	1.0	New document drafted	NA
08/15/2001	1.1	Debit card is added	
10/05/2001	1.2	Change of title for Purchasing Assistant	6.3, 7.2.3
	1.2	New Department Executive title	6.1

Explanation of Answer:

This example contains multiple errors for each line in the 'Revision History' table:

- *In row one, revision '1.0', the use of the word, 'Document' in the 'Change' column is not acceptable. Specify whether the document is a policy or procedure. In the 'Reference Section(s)' column, the use of 'NA' is not an acceptable abbreviation as the word, "Not Applicable" has not been used earlier. Another use of the first line of this table is the situation where a policy or procedure is completely rewritten. In this case, the change might read, 'Procedure converted to new format.'*

- *In row two, revision '1.1', the entry in the 'Change' column is short and not informative. The 'Change' description should be brief but meaningful. In addition, the 'Reference Section(s)' column should never be blank. Any indication of carelessness or poor writing can turn away a reader.*

- *In row three, revision '1.2,' the entry in the 'Change' column is not complete. When titles change, it is a good idea to include the 'to' and 'from' titles. In this example, the 'to' title is not specified. The section entries in the 'Reference Section(s)' column appear accurate except they are erroneous references. Use the "Search" or "Find" features of your word processor to find all references.*

- *In row four, revision '1.2,' a second title change has been added. Again, the method of showing a change in title is wrong. Additionally, though not wrong, there is no need to repeat the revision number for changes made on a single date.*

CHECKING YOUR WORK

Verify that the *Revision History* entries do not conflict with the "Common Mistakes." Verify the dates are working days. Policies and procedures are generally not released on nonworking days or holidays. Check that the revision number is recorded and is increased with each change. Verify that the change description is concise and makes sense. Double-check the section references to confirm their accuracy.

SUMMARY

The *Revision History* section is the second section of the WRITING FORMAT. This section serves the purpose of documenting all revision changes to a policy or procedure document (including the publication of a new document or a document that has been converted to this new WRITING FORMAT). The format for the *Revision History* is your choice. Pay attention to the information you insert into this section; the reader will thank you if the changes are easy to read and understand without further reading or analysis.

REFERENCES

Dobrian, Joseph, Business Writing Skills, AMACOM, New York, New York, 1998.

Page, Stephen B., Achieving 100% Compliance of Policies and Procedures, BookMasters, Inc., Mansfield, Ohio, 2000.

Page, Stephen B., Establishing a System of Policies and Procedures, BookMasters, Inc., Mansfield, Ohio, 1998.

Chapter 6

3.0 <u>Persons Affected</u>
Third Section, Writing Format

Objectives for this Chapter

- Describe the purpose of this third section and its importance to the WRITING FORMAT
- Provide a complete analysis of the "do's" and "don'ts" of the *Persons Affected* section
- Provide questions and suggested answers to your responses to the *Persons Affected* exercises

Topics Include:

Sample Template and WRITING FORMAT
Purpose of Section 3: <u>Persons Affected</u>
Format of <u>Persons Affected</u> Section
Common Mistakes
Scenario of <u>Persons Affected</u> Section
What to Look For
<u>Persons Affected</u> Exercise
Good Answers
"Not So Good" Answers
Checking your Work
Summary
References

A TEMPLATE AND A WRITING FORMAT

	Document No.	
	Effective Date	
	Revision Date	
TITLE OF POLICY or PROCEDURE	Revision No.	
	Page No.	
	Approval:	

1.0   Purpose

Describes objective(s) for writing a policy or procedure.

2.0   Revision History

Shows list of document changes to this document.

3.0   Persons Affected

Identifies the users of this document.

4.0   Policy

Describes the general organizational attitude of the company.

5.0   Definitions

Defines abbreviations, acronyms, forms, words infrequently used and technical terms.

6.0   Responsibilities

Summarizes the roles and responsibilities of all individuals involved with this document.

7.0   Procedures

Defines and outlines the rules, regulations, methods, timing, place, and personnel responsible for accomplishing the policy as stated in the *Policy* section above.

PURPOSE OF SECTION 3: <u>PERSONS AFFECTED</u>

This is the third section heading of the WRITING FORMAT. The *Persons Affected* section reflects the audience or targeted users that influence or support a specific policy or procedure. Every policy or procedure has some kind of audience, whether it is "all employees" or a single department.

FORMAT OF *<u>PERSONS AFFECTED</u>* SECTION

This is the <u>only</u> section where the actual wording of the section heading can vary. For instance, this section could be named: "Departments Affected" or "Employees Affected." The text that follows is typically a more specific listing, e.g., under "Departments Affected" it could read "Finance and Accounting" or "Purchasing, Receiving, and Accounting Departments."

In addition to statements about which entities are included, there can be a reason for including an exclusion statement. For instance, a specific policy or procedure might only affect the continental United States (48 states) and not Alaska and Hawaii. The section heading might read "Areas Affected," and the text could read, "The 48 states within the Continental United States." The exclusion sentence could read, "Alaska and Hawaii are excluded from this procedure."

The format of this section is typically a single fragmented sentence like "All Employees" or "All Sales Offices." In the case of a detailed explanation, both a paragraph and an outline style are acceptable. The choice is yours.

IS THE *<u>PERSONS AFFECTED</u>* SECTION REQUIRED OR OPTIONAL?

The *Persons Affected* section is required for policies and procedures. Making the assumption that the audience for policies and procedures is "All employees" is rarely a reality.

COMMON MISTAKES

The common mistakes for the *Persons Affected* section includes:

- Omitting the *Persons Affected* section
- Specifying *"All employees"* as the audience when the audience actually consists of a lesser number of groups or individuals
- Limiting an audience to several departments when the policy or procedure affects more departments, directly or indirectly

- Omitting exclusion statements when groups of people or departments are not intended to use a specific policy or procedure

SCENARIO OF THE _PERSONS AFFECTED_ SECTION

A scenario for the _Persons Affected_ section includes information collected during the research or prewriting step. While the audience of a policy or procedure may seem obvious, it is quite easy to overlook user groups that influence or are affected by a policy or procedure. In this section, you know the following:

- Employees who receive prior approval from management can initiate purchase requisitions for the purchase of MRO supply items
- The purchasing personnel involved with the purchasing process are purchasing managers, buyers, purchasing assistants, and clerks
- Support personnel outside of the purchasing department include the employees' managers, receiving clerks, inspectors, and accounting clerks
- Only purchasing departments in North America are included in this procedure and all other purchasing departments are excluded because they have their own predefined policies, procedures, and practices that conform to the standards of the country where they are located

WHAT TO LOOK FOR

Look for all the people and departments you have been working with during the research or prewriting step. During the coordination and review steps of the writing process, check for additional groups of people who influence or support a specific policy or procedure. Discuss the _Persons Affected_ section with those individuals that were originally identified during the research or prewriting step. Your goal is to identify all groups who influence or support a policy or procedure. The omission of any key groups could be disastrous to total buy-in.

PERSONS AFFECTED EXERCISE

Write four sentences identifying the audiences of the _Persons Affected_ section as follows: (1) include all employees authorized to make purchase requests, (2) include the job functions of individuals that will assist with the processing of purchase requests from receipt of a purchase requisition into the purchasing department to the payment of the invoice, (3) change the section heading to reflect "North American Purchasing Departments," and (4) write an exclusion statement for purchasing departments outside of North

America that do not have to follow the guidelines of this procedure. Record your answers on a notepad or word processor. Save your work.

GOOD ANSWER

3.0 <u>North American Purchasing Departments</u>

    3.1 All employees who are authorized in advance from their management to make purchase requests

    3.2 Purchasing managers, purchasing assistants, buyers, and purchasing clerks

    3.3 Receiving clerks, inspectors, and accounting clerks

    3.4 <u>Exclusion statement</u>: All purchasing departments outside of North America are specifically excluded from this procedure

<u>Explanation of Answer</u>:

The outline style was selected as the answer to this exercise due to the lengthy inclusion statements. A shortened version of this section might read, 'All employees authorized to initiate purchase requests; purchasing personnel; receiving personnel; inspection personnel, and accounting personnel.' While this fragmented sentence is wordy, it covers all of the applicable groups involved with this particular procedure. The amount of detail in this section is your choice. You will find that many of your policies and procedures contain short 'Persons Affected' statements like, 'For exempt employees only,' or 'All sales offices worldwide.'

This example includes a listing of the functions of those individuals, or groups of individuals, who initiate a purchase requisition, receive an order, inspect the received items, and pay an invoice. Second, the section heading was changed from 'Persons Affected' to 'North American Purchasing Departments.' Third, an exclusion statement was added as a precaution to ensure purchasing departments outside of North America do not think they have to follow the guidelines of this procedure.

If you still believe that there will be some confusion, you could add a second sentence to the exclusion statement. For example, 'Contact your Purchasing Manager for a copy of the relevant practices and procedures for your division or country,' or 'Contact the Procedure Department for details about policies and procedures written in other divisions.'

"NOT SO GOOD" ANSWER

3.0   <u>Persons Affected</u>

Applies to all employees.

<u>Explanation of Answer:</u>

The 'all employees' answer is a poor answer for these exercises. While you could argue that the 'all employees' statement is valid because any group of employees falls under the heading of 'all employees,' a specific audience selection is preferred. With a more focused audience, it will make it easier for the reader to understand the intent of a policy or procedure.

CHECKING YOUR WORK

Check your answers with the "Common Mistakes" section and make any necessary adjustments. Verify the functional titles you have selected with the information collected during the research or prewriting step. If you have any doubts, contact the Human Resources Department for a current organization chart or report that lists all employees by department and job title.

SUMMARY

The *Persons Affected* section is the third section of the WRITING FORMAT. This section identifies the audience of a specific policy or procedure. Fragmented sentences are an acceptable format for this section. Exclusion statements should be considered when there could be confusion as to the exact audience of a specific policy or procedure.

REFERENCES

Dobrian, Joseph, <u>Business Writing Skills</u>, AMACOM, New York, New York, 1998.

Page, Stephen B., <u>Achieving 100% Compliance of Policies and Procedures</u>, BookMasters, Inc., Mansfield, Ohio, 2000.

Page, Stephen B., <u>Establishing a System of Policies and Procedures</u>, BookMasters, Inc., Mansfield, Ohio, 1998.

Chapter 7

4.0 <u>Policy</u>
Fourth Section, Writing Format

Objectives for this Chapter

- Describe the purpose of this fourth section and its importance to the WRITING FORMAT
- Provide a complete analysis of the "do's" and "don'ts" of the *Policy* section
- Provide questions and suggested answers to your responses to the *Policy* exercises

Topics Include:

Sample Template and WRITING FORMAT
Purpose of Section 4: <u>Policy</u>
Format of <u>Policy</u> Section
Common Mistakes
Scenario of <u>Policy</u> Section
What to Look For
<u>Policy</u> Exercise
Good Answers
"Not So Good" Answers
Checking your Work
Summary
References

A TEMPLATE AND A WRITING FORMAT

	Document No.	
	Effective Date	
TITLE OF POLICY or PROCEDURE	Revision Date	
	Revision No.	
	Page No.	
	Approval:	

1.0 Purpose

Describes objective(s) for writing a policy or procedure.

2.0 Revision History

Shows list of document changes to this document.

3.0 Persons Affected

Identifies the users of this document.

4.0 Policy

Describes the general organizational attitude of the company.

5.0 Definitions

Defines abbreviations, acronyms, forms, words infrequently used and technical terms.

6.0 Responsibilities

Summarizes the roles and responsibilities of all individuals involved with this document.

7.0 Procedures

Defines and outlines the rules, regulations, methods, timing, place, and personnel responsible for accomplishing the policy as stated in the *Policy* section above.

PURPOSE OF SECTION 4: <u>POLICY</u>

This is the fourth section of the WRITING FORMAT. The *Policy* section is the most important section heading for a policy or procedure because it provides the objectives, strategies, goals, culture, and vision and mission of an organization as they relate to a specific policy or procedure. Even if you have made the decision to write a separate policy manual or to co-mingle policies and procedures in a single manual, a *Policy* section heading is still required in both a policy and procedure document. Refer to Chapter 1, "Importance of a Writing Format," for the rationale behind this comment.

Policy statements generally originate from the following kinds of information:

- Goals or objectives of senior management toward specific business processes or issues
- General company or department assumptions (i.e., facts taken for granted)
- Department guidelines for specific business processes or practices

FORMAT OF *POLICY* SECTION

The format of the *Policy* section can be an outline or paragraph format. If there is only one *Policy* statement, then a single sentence or paragraph written in a paragraph format will often suffice. When there are two or more *Policy* statements, then an outline format is preferred.

The *Policy* section should use a consistent opening phrase, as was the case in the *Purpose* section. The format choice is yours. My personal favorite opening phrase is "The policy of [your company name] is to ensure:" The colon indicates that several policy statements are forthcoming. If you have one *Policy* statement, then there is no need for the colon. If you have two or more policy statements, then retain the colon and list the statements in logical order using outline numbering. You should never use bullets because bullets cannot be clearly referenced. You can change the word *ensure* to a word of your choice but each statement thereafter should lead into a natural sentence structure. An example of a natural flowing sentence is shown in the exercises.

IS THIS *POLICY* SECTION REQUIRED OR OPTIONAL?

The *Policy* section is required for policies and procedures even if you are required by your management, or industry standards, to maintain a policy manual alongside a procedure manual. If you decide to make the *Policy* section optional when you also have a policy manual, it is recommended that you make a reference to the specific policy document (within the Policy Manual) from the *Policy, Definitions,* or *Procedures* sections of the procedure document. Your goal is to maintain the consistency of the WRITING FORMAT at all times.

COMMON MISTAKES

The common mistakes for the *Policy* section include:

- Omitting the *Policy* section heading from procedure documents
- Writing "Not Applicable" for the *Policy* section either in policy or procedure documents
- Using specific procedural statements instead of general policy statements
- Writing policy statements that do not support the main focus of the *Purpose* section
- Writing a policy statement that includes information that will not be supported by the procedural statements in the *Procedures* section (there is a possibility of writing too much information in this section)
- Failing to include a consistent opening phrase
- Using the passive voice in the opening phrase, or anywhere in the *Policy* section
- Using an unnatural word flow when listing policy statements after an opening phrase
- Failing to list all of the policy statements for either a policy or procedure document

SCENARIO OF THE <u>*POLICY*</u> SECTION

The source of policy information is different from the information collected for the other six sections. Policy information is generally collected during interviews with senior management including the Chief Executive Officer (CEO), the President, and the department executives (i.e., the highest person in a single department) of those departments listed in the *Persons Affected* section. Policy information can also be derived from existing company or department processes, policies, procedures, and practices. In this scenario, you know the following:

- Senior management believes that the purchasing professionals within the Purchasing Department are the only employees that can obligate suppliers and commit funds

- Purchasing Department's policy that the purchase requisition form is the only document acceptable for the purchase of MRO supply items
- Human Resources' policy that personal items cannot be procured or received by any employee on company premises

WHAT TO LOOK FOR

Look for the kind of statements that reflect decisions made by management. Refer to notes you gathered during interviews with management during the research or prewriting step. Look back at the *Purpose* statement for clues. Read the mission, vision, and policy statements published by any department that could influence the inputs or outputs of this policy or procedure. Review the *Policy* sections of the sample policies and procedures in Part 3.

POLICY EXERCISE

Write three policy statements plus an opening phrase that includes: (1) management's decision that only the purchasing department is authorized to obligate suppliers for orders from the company; (2) purchasing department's viewpoint that the purchase requisition form is the only acceptable method to request the purchase of MRO supply items; and (3) viewpoint of the Human Resources department on the purchase and receipt of personal items. Record your answers on a notepad or word processor. Save your work.

GOOD ANSWER

4.0   Policy

The policy of [insert your company name] is to ensure:

4.1   The purchasing department is the only department that is authorized to engage suppliers and obligate funds through purchase orders and contracts.

4.2   The purchase requisition form is the only document that will be accepted by the purchasing department for the procurement of MRO supply items.

4.3   Personal items (e.g., flowers, refreshments, personal subscriptions, or gifts) are not purchased on company premises or received by the company through the receiving department or any other entrance to the company or its properties.

<u>Explanation of Answer:</u>

This example reflects a typical policy statement. Check out the examples in Part 3 as an aid to understand these answers. Opening phrases in 'Policy' statements are generally used to introduce a listing of policy statements. This opening phrase can be reused in future policies or procedures. Each statement is a complete sentence when coupled with the opening phrase (i.e., natural flowing sentence), that is, when reading 'The policy of [insert your company name] is to ensure...' each sentence thereafter completes a thought and does not violate any grammar rules. The abbreviation, 'MRO,' can be used because it was defined in the title.

Policy statements outline the company's position or strategy for a policy or procedure. Each of the three statements expresses a fact derived from the strategy positions of the company and the purchasing department. Note that policy statements are typically written as 'statements of fact' rather than as processes or methods for accomplishing tasks.

You will learn from experience which kinds of statements belong in the 'Policy' section. Compare your policy statements from both your exercises and your actual policies and procedures with the sample policies and procedures contained in Part 3 of this book.

"NOT SO GOOD" ANSWER

4.0   <u>Policy</u>

It is the policy of [insert your company name] to:

4.1   Expenditures of company funds for goods and services are properly reviewed and approved.

4.2   The purchasing department is the only department that can accept purchase requests from employees.

4.3   Adhere to the policies of the HR Department pertinent to personal items.

<u>Explanation of Answer:</u>

Each policy statement is vague and not informative. While the opening phrase has been included, the wording is inappropriate. For instance, the phrase, 'It is the policy of [insert your company name] to...' has several *problems. First, the sentence starts with "It" and the reference is unclear. Second, two of the three sentences that follow the opening phrase are <u>not</u> natural flowing sentences (i.e., if you remove the colon, the sentence should form a complete thought and not violate any grammar rules).*

- *The first sentence, '4.1,' is not a complete thought when coupled with the opening phrase. This policy statement is not specific for purchasing activities; a statement should be rephrased to include a reference to the purchasing department and to the use of purchase orders and contracts.*

- *The second sentence, '4.2,' is not a complete thought when coupled with the opening phrase. Second, while a 'purchase request' might be referencing a purchase requisition form, it could also be interpreted as requests that are made through the telephone, email, fax, or as a walk-in, into the purchasing department. You should always try to write in specific terms (i.e., purchase requisitions) instead of general terms (i.e., purchase requests).*

- *The third sentence, '4.3,' is a complete sentence when coupled with the opening phrase. The abbreviation, 'HR,' should be spelled out because it has not been defined yet. In this instance, the term, 'HR,' is referring to the Human Resources Department. Second, problems exist with this sentence because the reader has been given information that will require further research. A short, descriptive summary of the Human Resources' policy on personal items is preferred over a vague statement that forces the reader to seek out information not contained in this document.*

Writing statements that are vague and not informative should be avoided because the reader will often not take the time to seek out additional information. This brings us to a legal question. If the reader is given all the information about a specific policy or procedure, the company can hold him accountable for his actions. If the reader is given vague information, then it is more difficult to hold the reader accountable because you cannot be certain that he has the correct information in his possession. Often a procedure writer will request that a manual holder sign that he has received a document.

CHECKING YOUR WORK

Check your *Policy* statements within the "Common Mistakes" section and resolve any conflicts. Reread the policy statements that follow an opening phrase to ensure they are natural flowing sentences. Recheck the information you collected during the research or prewriting step.

SUMMARY

This is the fourth section of the WRITING FORMAT. The *Policy* section is an important section because it eliminates the need for a separate Policy manual, and even a separate policy document. Policy statements set the stage for the *Procedures* section that will include the processes to help carry out the policy statements outlined in the *Policy* section.

REFERENCES

Dobrian, Joseph, Business Writing Skills, AMACOM, New York, New York, 1998.

Page, Stephen B., Achieving 100% Compliance of Policies and Procedures, BookMasters, Inc., Mansfield, Ohio, 2000.

Page, Stephen B., Establishing a System of Policies and Procedures, BookMasters, Inc., Mansfield, Ohio, 1998.

Chapter 8

5.0 <u>Definitions</u>
Fifth Section, Writing Format

Objectives for this Chapter

- Describe the purpose of this fifth section and its importance to the WRITING FORMAT
- Provide a complete analysis of the "do's" and "don'ts" of the *Definitions* section
- Provide questions and suggested answers to your responses to the *Definitions* exercises

Topics Include:

Sample Template and WRITING FORMAT
Purpose of Section 5: <u>Definitions</u>
Format of <u>Definitions</u> Section
Optional Documentation
Common Mistakes
Scenario of <u>Definitions</u> Section
What to Look For
<u>Definitions</u> Exercise
Good Answers
"Not So Good" Answers
Checking your Work
Summary
References

A TEMPLATE AND A WRITING FORMAT

TITLE OF POLICY or PROCEDURE	Document No.	
	Effective Date	
	Revision Date	
	Revision No.	
	Page No.	
	Approval:	

1.0 Purpose

Describes objective(s) for writing a policy or procedure.

2.0 Revision History

Shows list of document changes to this document.

3.0 Persons Affected

Identifies the users of this document.

4.0 Policy

Describes the general organizational attitude of the company.

5.0 Definitions

Defines abbreviations, acronyms, forms, words infrequently used and technical terms.

6.0 Responsibilities

Summarizes the roles and responsibilities of all individuals involved with this document.

7.0 Procedures

Defines and outlines the rules, regulations, methods, timing, place, and personnel responsible for accomplishing the policy as stated in the *Policy* section above.

PURPOSE OF SECTION 5: <u>DEFINITIONS</u>

This is the fifth section heading of the WRITING FORMAT. The *Definitions* section defines objects or terms like acronyms, abbreviations, forms, reports, flow diagrams, models, words infrequently used, or technical jargon. Definitions are needed in policies and procedures because you cannot assume that readers can understand your use of objects or terms. Even the most basic definitions should be included. For instance, not everyone will know that a PR is a purchase requisition, or that a PO is a purchase order. For instance, the term "PR" can also mean public relations while the term "PO" can also mean public opinion. At a minimum, you should define the major words, phrases, terms, or objects that could be confusing your selected audience(s). Always consider defining the objects or terms used in your title, purpose, and policy statements; these definitions can often mean the difference between understanding and not understanding the focus of a policy or procedure.

<u>My advice to you</u>: Define any term or object that could possibly be misinterpreted. Use the following as alternatives: Look through a thesaurus - if there are several possible interpretations of a word, then define the word in the *Definitions* section.

FORMAT OF *DEFINITIONS* SECTION

Definitions are generally placed in order of importance, starting with the most important, or most referenced, definition first. A definition can be explained as "a method for developing a meaningful sentence or paragraph in which an object or term is defined." In general, a definition identifies the term to be defined and uses terminology suitable for the audience. The easiest way to define a term is to summarize its meaning in a simple sentence, much the way a dictionary does. Other times, a full-length paragraph may be necessary. In some cases, added information like benefits, examples, and reference material (e.g., forms, diagrams, models, or text that does not fit within the body of a policy or procedure) will help the reader understand a definition. When optional documentation is included in a policy or procedure, a short summary must be included in the *Definitions* section along with a reference to its location.

OPTIONAL DOCUMENTATION

Optional documentation is common for procedure documents but infrequent for policy documents. While you might be thinking, "Why not include an eighth section?" An extra section is not an option because it would add inconsistency to the standard WRITING FORMAT. Optional documentation is best handled as a reference from the *Definitions* or *Procedures* section. Optional documentation is placed at the end of a policy or procedure or referenced to an external location.

Optional documentation includes documents, forms, flow charts, diagrams, cumbersome text, or other content where an earlier reference has indicated that the reader would find that information in an appendix (i.e., supplementary material attached to the end of a document). For instance, if a reference reads, "Refer to Appendix A for a form sample and form instructions," the reader would expect to find Appendix A immediately following the *Procedures* section.

FORMAT OF OPTIONAL DOCUMENTATION

Each document should be placed in a separate appendix using the same template as in the policy or procedure. The word, "Appendix" plus a "[reference letter]," (e.g., Appendix "A"), should be centered at the top of the page. The body of the document should follow. I prefer this method to just attaching documents without regard to format; it provides an element of consistency when the reader sees all of the information of a policy or procedure contained within the borders of a single template. When including printed forms, the forms should be reduced to fit within the borders of the template. This can be accomplished by reducing the printed forms on a photocopy to fit within the borders.

For optional documentation, not included at the end of a policy or procedure, seek out the "referenced" document to make sure it is easy to locate. Readers will become quickly frustrated if they go to the effort of searching for a reference that either cannot be quickly found or does not exist.

Some readers may question placing forms at the end of a policy or procedure because forms add extra pages to a document and could make the document cumbersome. While this practice can add extra work to the job of a procedure writer, I believe it is a worthwhile effort. Users do not usually go to the effort of finding the most current version of a form; they will use whatever is convenient (e.g., old forms in their desk drawer or in a stationery cabinet). A policy or procedure is an excellent place to include pictures of forms and form instructions. Inexperienced writers tend to overlook form instructions. If a reader sees a picture of the correct form, the chances of the correct form being used increase, and hence, higher compliance can be achieved. A secondary benefit is that the reader does not have to seek out other sources to find form instructions.

For network or web policies and procedures, you have more flexibility in the manner in which you display optional documentation (i.e., there is no reason to be confined to the limited space within a template because you can "hyperlink" to almost any document or web address from electronically displayed documents on a network or web site).

IS THE *DEFINITIONS* SECTION REQUIRED OR OPTIONAL?

The *Definitions* section is required for all policies and procedures. The WRITING FORMAT remains the same. If a policy document has no definitions, then the words, "Not Applicable," should be entered. Eliminating the section heading is not an option.

COMMON MISTAKES

The common mistakes for the *Definitions* section include:

- Omitting the *Definitions* section
- Omitting the words, "Not Applicable," or leaving this section blank for policy or procedure documents
- Writing lengthy definitions instead of summary paragraphs with reference statements
- Failing to write definitions for terms, objects, acronyms, or abbreviations
- Failing to write reference statements at the end of a definition for objects like forms, models, or diagrams
- Failing to include copies of forms and form instructions at the end of a policy or procedure, or a reference to an external location
- Writing definitions about forms or documents with reference statements and then failing to include the optional documentation at the end of the policy or procedure or failing to include a reference to an external location
- Failing to include the correct reference (e.g., referencing Appendix B when it should have been Appendix A) for optional documentation

SCENARIO OF THE *DEFINITIONS* SECTION

The scenario for the *Definitions* section includes a list of objects or terms pertinent to this procedure. Objects or terms for this exercise include:

- Term: Maintenance, Repair, and Operating (MRO) Supply Items
- Object: Purchase Requisition (PR)
- Object: Request for Quotation (RFQ)

WHAT TO LOOK FOR

Check for keywords in your flow chart and task list that the audience may not readily recognize or understand. Use a thesaurus to identify words that could be easily confused. Use a dictionary to double-check your definitions. Look at the inputs and outputs of the flow chart as a possible source of terms or objects that could be defined. Review your definitions – there could be terms or objects within the definitions themselves that should also be defined or referenced.

DEFINITIONS EXERCISE

Write three definitions for the following: (1) maintenance, repair, and operating (MRO) supply items, (2) purchase requisition (PR) form - include a reference statement for the PR to an external forms catalogue, and (3) request for quotation (RFQ) form – include a reference statement for the RFQ to the end of this procedure. Record your answers on a notepad or word processor. Save your work.

GOOD ANSWER

5.0   Definitions

      5.1   Maintenance, Repair, and Operating (MRO) Supply Items. Expensed materials used by employees to help them perform their jobs. These materials can include, but are not limited to, small tools, cleaning supplies, office supplies, and a variety of other consumable items that are not-for-resale, not for production purposes, and cost less than $500.00.

      5.2   Purchase Requisition (PR). This document is a three-part, pre-numbered, form used by employees to request the purchase of materials or services by the purchasing department. The purchase requisition is the key document authorizing the purchasing department to buy specific materials, parts, supplies, equipment, and services. A purchase requisition describes what is to be purchased, provides a record of the purchase requisition, and approves the commitment of funds.

             Completion of the purchase requisition alone does not constitute placing an order. Refer to the latest forms catalogue maintained by the forms management department for a sample form and form instructions.

5.3 <u>Request for Quotation (RFQ)</u>. This document is a three-part, pre-numbered, form used by the purchasing department to request bids from suppliers. A request for quotation is a means of inviting bids from prospective suppliers. This form is the buyer's first official contact with possible suppliers. The quality and content of the RFQ can determine the outcome of the bidding process because it sets the stage for discussions and negotiations. Refer to Appendix A for a sample form and form instructions.

<u>Explanation of Answer</u>:

Each of these three definitions is clear in meaning and includes the appropriate references and details to establish an explicit definition. Reference sentences are included for each form (i.e., an object).

- *In '5.1' the 'Maintenance, Repair, and Operating (MRO) Supply Items' term is correctly defined; examples of supply items have also been included. Dollar limits have been set for using the form. The abbreviation, 'MRO,' has been properly defined – it can now be freely used anywhere from this point forward. No reference has been included because terms generally do not contain additional information that would require a reference.*

- *In '5.2' the 'Purchase Requisition' is defined. While this information is defined in detail in the 'Procedures' section, I prefer to give the reader more detail up front than to assume he will read the 'Procedures' section and find this same information. More detail enhances comprehension for the reader. Note that a reference statement has been included, pointing the reader to an external forms catalogue maintained by the forms management department, for a copy of the referenced form and form instructions.*

  When a form is involved, the procedure writer should coordinate the writing of a procedure with the forms management department to ensure that the design of the form and the form instructions do not contradict with the details of the procedure.

- *In '5.3' the 'Request for Quotation' form is defined. Again, the detail of the definition is your choice. A reference statement has been included as the last sentence of the definition because an object was being defined. The reader is pointed to the end of the procedure for a copy of the referenced form and form instructions.*

"NOT SO GOOD" ANSWER

5.0 <u>Definitions</u>

    5.1   <u>Maintenance, Repair, and Operating Supplies (MRO).</u> Supplies used by employees in the execution of their jobs. Examples include small tools, cleaning supplies, and office supplies.

    5.2   <u>Purchase Requisition (PR).</u> Form used by employees to purchase materials or services.

    5.3   <u>Request for Quotation.</u> Quotation form used by the purchasing department to obtain bids from suppliers. Refer to Appendix B for a sample form.

<u>Explanation of Answer:</u>

While these three definitions are passable, each definition contains several common errors.

- *In '5.1' the definition is short, concise, and contains examples. Still, the definition has three problems. First, the abbreviation, 'MRO,' should be placed after the phrase, 'maintenance, repair, and operating,' not at the end of the phrase. Second, the word, 'supplies' is used to define itself. Third, the second sentence is a fragmented sentence. Fragmented sentences should not be used in the 'Definitions' section.*

- *In '5.2' the definition of the purchase requisition is vague and not informative. A description of the physical characteristics of the PR should be included as well as the purpose of the form. In addition, the reference to the location of the object is not included.*

- *In '5.3' the definition of the 'request for quotation' form is concise but contains several errors. First, the abbreviation, 'RFQ,' is omitted and should be placed after the object, 'Request for Quotation.' Second, the word, 'quotation,' is used to define itself. Third, the reference to the location of a copy of the current form is incorrect or it suggests (as is the case) that an earlier reference was not included. Recall that the reference statement in '5.2' was omitted. This definition pointed to 'Appendix B' when an 'Appendix A' has yet to be identified.*

CHECKING YOUR WORK

Check for words and phrases used in the first four sections of the WRITING FORMAT – if they are not self-explanatory, then they should be defined in the *Definitions* section. Check the definitions and determine if you have words within your definitions that should also be defined. Double-check that you have included reference statements. Verify that you have included the referenced document either at the end of the procedure or at your designated external location.

SUMMARY

The importance of the *Definitions* section cannot be overemphasized. Inexperienced procedure writers tend to exclude definitions because they think their audience should understand the basic terms or objects of a specific policy or procedure. If there is the slightest doubt that a term or object will be misunderstood, it should be defined in the *Definitions* section and used in the *Procedures* section. A definition of a term or object serves no purpose if the term or object is not later explained in the *Procedures* section and in the case of an object, referenced at the end of a specific policy or procedure, or at an external location.

REFERENCES

Dobrian, Joseph, Business Writing Skills, AMACOM, New York, New York, 1998.

Page, Stephen B., Achieving 100% Compliance of Policies and Procedures, BookMasters, Inc., Mansfield, Ohio, 2000.

Page, Stephen B., Establishing a System of Policies and Procedures, BookMasters, Inc., Mansfield, Ohio, 1998.

Chapter 9

6.0 <u>Responsibilities</u>
Sixth Section, Writing Format

Objectives for this Chapter

- Describe the purpose of this sixth section and its importance to the WRITING FORMAT
- Provide a complete analysis of the "do's" and "don'ts" of the *Responsibilities* section
- Provide questions and suggested answers to your responses to the *Responsibility* exercises

Topics Include:

Sample Template and WRITING FORMAT
Purpose of Section 6: <u>Responsibilities</u>
Format of <u>Responsibilities</u> Section
Common Mistakes
Scenario of <u>Responsibilities</u> Section
What to Look For
<u>Responsibilities</u> Exercise
Good Answers
"Not So Good" Answers
Checking your Work
Summary
References

A TEMPLATE AND A WRITING FORMAT

		Document No.	
		Effective Date	
		Revision Date	
TITLE OF POLICY or PROCEDURE		Revision No.	
		Page No.	
		Approval:	

1.0   Purpose

Describes objective(s) for writing a policy or procedure.

2.0   Revision History

Shows list of document changes to this document.

3.0   Persons Affected

Identifies the users of this document.

4.0   Policy

Describes the general organizational attitude of the company.

5.0   Definitions

Defines abbreviations, acronyms, forms, words infrequently used and technical terms.

6.0   Responsibilities

Summarizes the roles and responsibilities of all individuals involved with this document.

7.0   Procedures

Defines and outlines the rules, regulations, methods, timing, place, and personnel responsible for accomplishing the policy as stated in the *Policy* section above.

PURPOSE OF SECTION 6: <u>RESPONSIBILITIES</u>

This is the sixth section of the WRITING FORMAT. The *Responsibilities* section is a summary listing that describes the roles and responsibilities of the individuals, or group, that performs actions in a policy or procedure. The *Procedures* section will provide the details behind the roles and responsibilities listed in this section. The *Responsibilities* section should be written in the same sequence of events that occurs under the *Procedures* section. Often the procedure writer should write the *Procedures* section <u>before</u> the *Responsibilities* section.

FORMAT OF *RESPONSIBILITIES* SECTION

The *Responsibilities* section is written as summary statements such as "All employees are required to..." or "Each sales office is responsible for..." There are two formats for the *Responsibilities* section. First, a single paragraph can be used if you only have one individual, or group, that is involved with a policy or procedure. Second, an outline format can be used if two or more individuals influence or support a policy or procedure. In both cases, summary statements are written. The details of the actions of those individuals, or groups, can then be included in the *Procedures* section.

The first sentence of a *Responsibilities* section is reserved for the individual who oversees the compliance of a policy or procedure. This person is responsible for resolving any conflicts, issues, or concerns an employee might have with a specific policy or procedure. The assigned person of this "compliance" role should be in a position that manages all of the functional areas of a specific policy or procedure. I used to ask the Chief Executive Officer (CEO) or President of the Company to sign all policies and procedures. The "CEO" rationale is simple; the CEO or President of the Company is not likely to be challenged. A compliance statement could read, "The CEO shall ensure compliance to this procedure."

The compliance statement sets the stage: The sentences that follow should contain the roles and responsibilities of those individuals, or groups, performing actions to carry out the intent of a specific policy or procedure. The actual names of the individuals should not be used.

IS THE *RESPONSIBILITIES* SECTION REQUIRED OR OPTIONAL?

The *Responsibilities* Section is required for all policies and procedures. At a minimum, you must include a "compliance" statement as the first sentence, to ensure a person, or group, takes full accountability for this specific policy or procedure.

COMMON MISTAKES

The common mistakes for the *Responsibilities* section include:

- Omitting the *Responsibilities* section
- Writing the words, "Not Applicable," in the *Responsibilities* section
- Failing to include a compliance statement as the first sentence of this section
- Writing the *Responsibilities* section in a different sequence than entered for the action statements in the *Procedures* section
- Writing procedural statements in the *Responsibilities* section
- Using a paragraph format instead of an outline style when there are two or more individuals, or groups, performing actions
- Entering responsibility statements in the passive voice instead of the active voice
- Writing actual names of persons instead of their roles or functions

SCENARIO OF THE *RESPONSIBILITIES* SECTION

The source of information for the *Responsibilities* section is derived from the two reference documents: Flow chart and task list. For these exercises, you know the following:

- The Purchasing Department Director oversees the purchasing process
- Employees initiate and prepare purchase requisitions for MRO supply items
- Employees coordinate management and accounting approval of their purchase requisitions
- The purchasing assistant reviews incoming purchase requisitions
- The purchasing manager reviews purchase requisitions upon receipt from the purchasing assistant and assigns the appropriate MRO buyer

WHAT TO LOOK FOR

Look for all individuals, groups of individuals, or departments that perform some kind of action, e.g., adhere to guidelines, select a form, review a form, approve or disapprove a form, sign and date a form, assign a person to perform another task, send out mail, receive a package, inspect an item, enter information into a log or computer, or deliver received items to an employee.

If you have completed the task list, the statements within the *Responsibilities* section should be straightforward to write.

RESPONSIBILITIES EXERCISE

Write four *Responsibility* statements using the following information: (1) the purchasing director is the person who is accountable for the compliance of this procedure; (2) the actions an employee should take when preparing a purchase requisition form; (3) the actions performed by a purchasing assistant when reviewing incoming purchase requisitions; and (4) the action of a purchasing manager when reviewing purchase requisitions submitted from the purchasing assistant. Record your answers on a notepad or word processor. Save your work.

GOOD ANSWER

6.0 Responsibilities

6.1 The Purchasing Department Director is responsible for ensuring compliance to this procedure.

6.2 Employees are expected to select the current purchase requisition and adhere to the guidelines of this procedure when requesting MRO supply items.

6.3 The purchasing assistant shall review all incoming purchase requisitions to ensure they are completed in accordance with current purchasing policies and procedures.

6.4 The purchasing manager shall review those purchase requisitions received from the purchasing assistant.

Explanation of Answer:

There were four roles stated in this exercise; therefore, the outline format was selected. Your style of writing will determine the detail of your policies and procedures.

- *In '6.1' the compliance statement is sufficient. You could write a more detailed statement like, 'The purchasing director shall ensure compliance to this procedure and serve as the person who will resolve any procedural conflicts that might arise.'*

- *In '6.2', '6.3, and '6.4' each responsibility statement has a summary-level topic sentence. The details behind the action statements should be written in the 'Procedures' section.*

"NOT SO GOOD" ANSWER

6.0   Responsibilities

    6.1   Donald Crawford, purchasing department director, shall ensure compliance to this procedure.

    6.2   It is the responsibility of employees to complete a purchase requisition when requesting small tools and office supplies.

    6.3   The purchasing assistant within the purchasing department shall review all requisitions. The purchasing assistant shall initial the purchase requisition in the lower-right hand corner of the requisition.

    6.4   Purchasing managers are responsible for making sure that all employees adhere to the guidelines of this procedure.

Explanation of Answer:

While these 'Responsibilities' statements appear to be summary statements, each statement has one or more errors.

- *In '6.1' the actual name, 'Donald Crawford,' does not belong in a policy or procedure. If the term, 'purchasing department director,' is referring to a specific person, then the initial letter of each word should be capitalized. Otherwise, lowercase will suffice.*

- *In '6.2' there are two errors. First, a sentence should not begin with 'it' because the reference is not clear. Second, the writer has limited the employee's choices of supply items. The scope should be broadened to include all MRO supply items.*

- *In '6.3' there are three errors. First, there is no need to mention the department where the purchasing assistant works. Second, the correct term to use is 'purchase requisition' or 'PR' not just 'requisition.' Purchase requisitions are not the only kind of requisitions in a company. There are other requisitions such as material and personnel requisitions. Third, the second sentence is a detail and it belongs in the 'Procedures' section.*

- *In '6.4' the statement is valid but redundant. The Purchasing Department Director (Section 6.1) is responsible for assuring compliance, not the purchasing managers. While the purchasing manager also has a 'compliance' responsibility, the purchasing manager has more specific roles and responsibilities that should be mentioned in this section. Your goal is to write clear and concise sentences.*

CHECKING YOUR WORK

Check that the action statements in the *Responsibilities* section parallel the general flow of the actions within the *Procedures* section. Revisit the common mistakes section and make any appropriate adjustments. Double-check the flow chart and task list to ensure you have identified the actions performed by all individuals, or groups, that influence or support a policy or procedure. Confirm that only the roles and responsibilities of individuals are included in the *Responsibilities* section and that the *Responsibilities* statements are at the summary level and do not contain detail that should be included in the *Procedures* section.

SUMMARY

The *Responsibilities* section is the sixth section of the WRITING FORMAT. The purpose of this section is to write summary-level statements of those individuals performing actions in a policy or procedure. The first sentence of the *Responsibilities* section contains the "compliance" statement; this is one of the most important statements to include in any policy or procedure. Otherwise, policies and procedures could fail because there would be no one to hold "users" accountable for their actions.

REFERENCES

Dobrian, Joseph, Business Writing Skills, AMACOM, New York, New York, 1998.

Page, Stephen B., Achieving 100% Compliance of Policies and Procedures, BookMasters, Inc., Mansfield, Ohio, 2000.

Page, Stephen B., Establishing a System of Policies and Procedures, BookMasters, Inc., Mansfield, Ohio, 1998.

Chapter 10

7.0 <u>Procedures</u>
Seventh Section, Writing Format

Objectives for this Chapter

- Describe the purpose of this seventh section and its importance to the WRITING FORMAT
- Provide a complete analysis of the "do's" and "don'ts" of the *Procedures* section
- Provide exercises and suggested answers to questions posed in the *Procedures* exercises

Topics Include:

Sample Template and WRITING FORMAT
Purpose of Section 7: <u>Procedures</u>
Format of <u>Procedures</u> Section
Common Mistakes
Scenario of <u>Procedures</u> Section
What to Look For
<u>Procedures</u> Exercise
Good Answers
"Not So Good" Answers
Checking your Work
Summary
References

A TEMPLATE AND A WRITING FORMAT

	Document No.	
	Effective Date	
	Revision Date	
TITLE OF POLICY or PROCEDURE	Revision No.	
	Page No.	
	Approval:	

1.0   Purpose

Describes objective(s) for writing a policy or procedure.

2.0   Revision History

Shows list of document changes to this document.

3.0   Persons Affected

Identifies the users of this document.

4.0   Policy

Describes the general organizational attitude of the company.

5.0   Definitions

Defines abbreviations, acronyms, forms, words infrequently used and technical terms.

6.0   Responsibilities

Summarizes the roles and responsibilities of all individuals involved with this document.

7.0   Procedures

Defines and outlines the rules, regulations, methods, timing, place, and personnel responsible for accomplishing the policy as stated in the *Policy* section above.

PURPOSE OF SECTION 7: <u>PROCEDURES</u>

This is the seventh and last section of the WRITING FORMAT. The *Procedures* section defines and outlines the rules, regulations, methods, timing, place, and personnel responsible for accomplishing the policy statements as outlined in the *Policy* section. The steps from the flow chart and task list are outlined in a general sequence from start to finish in the *Procedures* section.

FORMAT OF *PROCEDURES* SECTION

The format of the *Procedures* section is generally laid out in an outline style. While a single paragraph format is sufficient for short procedures, a list of unnumbered paragraphs is not acceptable. By using the flow chart and task list as references, the procedure writer can write the procedure statements in a logical sequence laid out in an outline format. The paragraph format should be avoided because it can be the root of potential problems and inconsistencies. Recall my personal example where the procedure manager unknowingly buried important points in lengthy paragraphs.

IS THIS *PROCEDURES* SECTION REQUIRED OR OPTIONAL?

The *Procedures* section is required for all procedure documents but is optional for policy documents. The primary focus of a procedure is the *Procedures* section; the primary focus of a policy is the *Policy* section. For consistency purposes, the *Procedures* section heading is retained in a policy document. The words, "Not Applicable," should be written in this section when the *Procedures* section does not apply in a policy document. The sample Policy document in Part 3 of this book, contains a *Procedures* section.

COMMON MISTAKES

The common mistakes for the *Procedures* section include:

- Omitting this section for a policy document
- Failing to write, "Not Applicable," in the *Procedures* section for a policy document if the procedural statements are not needed
- Failing to write procedural statements that carry out the intent of the policy statements in the *Policy* section
- Using the paragraph format instead of the outline style when there are two or more procedural statements
- Writing procedural statements that do not follow the sequence of the referenced flow chart and task list

- Failing to verify that the action statements within the *Responsibilities* section parallel the action statements within the *Procedures* section
- Failing to write the necessary details to support the summary statements of the *Responsibilities* section
- Writing policy statements in the *Procedures* section
- Failing to include the terms or objects that were defined in the *Definitions* section

SCENARIO OF THE _PROCEDURES_ SECTION

A scenario for the *Procedures* section includes any information collected during the prewriting or research step. While the flow chart and task list are the primary inputs to this section, any other information collected from interviews, workshops, surveys, emails, questionnaires, or white papers, should be included. For these exercises, you know the following:

- The type of demand that triggers an employee to prepare a purchase requisition
- The process the employee performs when preparing a purchase requisition and obtaining management and accounting approval
- The process the purchasing department performs upon receipt of a purchase requisition from an employee
- The specific processes taken by the purchasing assistant, purchasing manager, buyer, and purchasing clerk when processing a purchase requisition, and generating a purchase order
- The actions the receiving department takes upon receipt of a copy of a purchase order from the purchasing department, including the generation of a receiver document and the processes required to process an incoming order from a supplier

WHAT TO LOOK FOR

Look for information you gathered from: interviews with business process owners, users, customers, managers, and others involved with the purchasing process. Double-check that you have identified all relevant sequence steps of the flow chart and task list. Reread the current policies, procedures, forms, and form instructions of the purchasing, receiving, and accounting departments.

PROCEDURES EXERCISE

Write three procedural statements based on the following information: (1) steps an employee takes to prepare and process a purchase requisition, (2) the actions of the purchasing assistant perform when processing an incoming purchase requisition, and (3) the actions of the receiving clerks upon receipt of copy of the purchase order from the purchasing department. Record your answers on a notepad or word processor. Save your work.

GOOD ANSWER

7.0   Procedures

    7.1   Any authorized employee can create a purchase requisition to purchase Maintenance, Repair, and Operating (MRO) supply items in accordance with the requirements referenced in this procedure.

        7.1.1   The employee should normally view several catalogues or past department orders to get an estimate of the total order value of the items being requested on the purchase requisition. This research will aid the employee and his management in deciding if the items being requested are a useful purchase for the department.

        7.1.2   The employee shall obtain the latest version of the purchase requisition form from the forms stock or designated location for the forms inventory.

        7.1.3   The employee should complete the purchase requisition and forward it to his manager for approval. Upon approval, the employee should forward the purchase requisition to the accounting department for budget and signature approval.

        7.1.4   When the accounting department returns the purchase requisition to the employee, the purchase requisition can be mailed, hand-carried, or faxed to the purchasing department for order placement. Emails and electronic signatures are unacceptable.

    7.2   A purchasing assistant will review all incoming purchase requisitions to ensure compliance with the guidelines contained in this procedure.

7.2.1 The purchasing assistant will ensure that the department and accounting signatures are correct and that all fields on the purchase requisition have been properly completed in accordance with the form instructions included at the end of this procedure.

7.2.2 Upon approval, the purchasing assistant will initial the purchase requisition at the bottom right corner and forward it to the appropriate purchasing manager for review, approval, and assignment of an MRO buyer. In the infrequent case that the Purchase Requisition (PR) is disapproved, the purchasing assistant will make two attempts to contact the employee. If the employee cannot be reached, or if the problem cannot be resolved over the telephone or with email, then the PR will be returned to the employee for correction.

7.3 Upon receipt of a copy of the purchase order, a clerical person within the receiving department will copy the purchase order onto a pre-collated, four-part set of colored paper to produce a "Receiver." This document will be used to receive and acknowledge the receipt of supply items.

7.3.1 The Receiver is filed in the receiving department with the applicable PO copy.

7.3.2 Upon receipt of the items ordered, the receiving department will match the order received to the packing sheet provided by the supplier and to the Receiver. The receiving information is recorded on the Receiver and any discrepancies are noted. Depending on the terms and conditions of the purchase order, the inspection department might get involved with the order. If the order passes inspection, the order is forwarded to the requesting employee, and the order is distributed as follows:

7.3.2.1 Copy 1 is forwarded to the applicable buyer.

7.3.2.2 Copies 2 and 3 are forwarded to the accounting department.

7.3.2.3 Copy 4 is retained by the receiving department.

Explanation of Answer:

This answer contains the right amount of detail for a typical procedure. More detail is also acceptable. If you only write summary-level procedure statements, the reader may not fully understand the intent of the procedure. The amount of detail is your choice. The 'Procedures' section has been written in the outline format because there are two or more procedural steps included in the flow chart.

In '7.1, 7.2, 7.3' the first sentence of each section introduces the reader to the topic of the paragraph (i.e., the exercise for this section). Each statement that follows, supports the topic of the higher level heading or subheading. For instance, sections '7.2.1' and '7.2.2' support the topic introduced in '7.2.' This kind of supporting evidence for a topic sentence is good practice. Each heading, e.g., 7.1, 7.2, and 7.3, has at least two subheadings. The use of only one subheading is poor practice and should be avoided.

"NOT SO GOOD" ANSWER

7.0   Procedures

    7.1   Requesters will submit a purchase requisition form to his manager for approval. Upon approval, the requisition form will be forwarded to the purchasing department.

    7.2   The purchasing department will receive all purchase requisitions into their department where they will be reviewed for accuracy.

    7.3   The receiving department will use a receiver to process items that are received from the supplier filling the order. The receiver is distributed in accordance with the distribution list printed at the bottom of the receiving document.

Explanation of Answer:

While these three procedure statements provide adequate responses to the exercises, each statement contains one or more errors. Note that these answers do not contain enough detail. The two primary references, the flow chart and task list, contain sequence steps that should be described in detail, not omitted. The more information the reader has about a specific policy or procedure, the better chance he will adhere to its guidelines.

- *In '7.1' there are four errors. First, the term, 'requesters,' is a poor choice because the word has not been used in the procedure. Second, the event that causes the employee to initiate a purchase requisition should be described. Third, the term, 'requisition,' is incomplete; the modifier, 'purchase,' is necessary to avoid confusion as to the type of requisition used. Fourth, there is no indication as to who will forward the purchase requisition to the purchasing department.*

- *In '7.2' there are three errors. First, there is no indication as to who in the purchasing department will accept and review the incoming purchase requisitions. Second, there is no indication how and by what standards (i.e., reference to a current policy or procedure) the purchase requisition will be reviewed. Third, there is no mention of what happens when a purchase requisition is accepted or rejected.*

- *In '7.3' these two sentences are adequate though the source of the receiver is not clear. Additionally, there is no indication how the receiver is used when items are received.*

CHECKING YOUR WORK

Check your procedure statements with the flow chart and task list you created during the research or prewriting step. Verify that the *Procedures* section contains statements that carry out the intent of the policy statements in the *Policy* statement. Double-check that the *Procedures* section has been written in a logical flow from start to finish.

SUMMARY

The *Procedures* section is very important to a procedure document because the processes are laid out in a sequential and logical order. The level of detail usually depends on your writing style, current practices on writing policies and procedures, expectations of the readers, and the culture.

REFERENCES

Page, Stephen B., <u>Achieving 100% Compliance of Policies and Procedures</u>, BookMasters, Inc., Mansfield, Ohio, 2000.

Page, Stephen B., <u>Establishing a System of Policies and Procedures</u>, BookMasters, Inc., Mansfield, Ohio, 1998.

Chapter 11

Writing Format Checklist

Objectives for this Chapter

- Describe how the seven sections of the WRITING FORMAT fit together
- Show how a "Writing Format Checklist" can be used to verify that the common mistakes in Chapters 4 to 10 have been isolated and corrected

Topics Include:

Congratulations: You Made It!
Putting it all Together
Writing Format Checklist
References

CONGRATULATIONS: YOU MADE IT!

If you have done all the exercises, you are on the road to developing a new and improved writing skill for drafting policy and procedure documents. A checklist is provided in this chapter to assist you with the review of your final policy or procedure documents. In addition, you should refer to the "Editing Checklist" from Chapter 2 once more. Use both checklists when doing a final review of your draft policies and procedures. Develop your own exercises and use them for training employees new to writing policies and procedures. Introduce this book at team meetings when discussing a new policy or procedure topic or when asking for assistance with the drafting or editing of your documents. Make copies of Chapters 4 through 10 and distribute them to team members and "would-be" procedure writers to assist you with the prewriting and writing steps of the writing process. With time, patience, and skill, you will soon be writing great policies and procedures. Your reader will thank you. Reread the book, redo the exercises, and make copies of the checklists for future use.

PUTTING IT ALL TOGETHER

Whether you have written the seven sections of the WRITING FORMAT sequentially or randomly, once you have completed the sections, you will have a draft policy or procedure ready for editing and review. Recall that there is only one sequence for policies and procedures.

1.0	Purpose
2.0	Revision History
3.0	Persons Affected
4.0	Policy
5.0	Definitions
6.0	Responsibilities
7.0	Procedures

WRITING FORMAT CHECKLIST

The "Writing Format Checklist" is being introduced as a method of double-checking and auditing the writing style, headings, subheadings, paragraphs, sentences, and words of each section of the WRITING FORMAT to ensure consistency and standardization of format and content. The questions for the checklist are derived from the "Common Mistakes" sections from Chapters 4 through 10. Use this checklist after you complete your first draft of your policies and procedures, and after each subsequent draft.

The checklist contains more than 40 questions. Each question has been phrased to accept a "Yes" answer if you are doing the step correctly. If you answer "No," you are <u>not</u> doing the step correctly. While I have included a place for "Not Applicable" (NA), I think you should have an excellent reason for using, 'NA.' For any answer other than "Yes," revisit the referenced chapter for ways to correct your answers and turn them into "Yes" answers.

Writing Format Checklist			
Chapter	**Question**	**Yes**	**No/NA**
Chapters 1-2	Did you use the WRITING FORMAT presented in this book? To continue, the answer must be "yes."		
	Have you included all seven steps?		
	Did you keep the names of the seven section headings the same (except for *Persons Affected*)?		
	Did you refer to the "Editing Checklist" at least once during the review and editing process of a specific policy or procedure?		
Chapter 4	Do you have a *Purpose* section heading?		
	Does your *Purpose* statement reflect the objective or goal of your policy or procedure?		
	Is your *Purpose* statement brief yet comprehensive?		
	Have you written your *Purpose* statement with abbreviations, acronyms, or technical terms that are not defined yet?		
	Have you used an opening phrase that is consistent from policy to policy or procedure to procedure?		
Chapter 5	Do you have a *Revision History* section?		
	Did you update the *Revision History* for each change that was made, no matter how minor?		
	Did you write brief, yet meaningful, change descriptions?		
	Did you increment each revision number?		
	Did you find all the references to identified changes?		
Chapter 6	Do you have a *Persons Affected* section?		
	Did you include all known audiences that support or are impacted by a specific policy or procedure?		

	Did you limit your audiences only to those that are involved with a policy or procedure?		
	If you included an exclusion statement, does it make sense when read with the accompanying inclusion statement(s)?		
Chapter 7	Did you include a *Policy* section for your policy or procedure?		
	Did you write the *Policy* statement based on the mission, vision, goals, general attitude, and culture of the company?		
	Do your policy statements support the main focus of the *Purpose* section?		
	Did you write general statements instead of procedural statements?		
	Did you use an opening phrase?		
	Did you write natural flowing sentences following the opening phrase?		
	Did you use the active voice instead of the passive voice?		
	If there is one policy statement, did you write the statement in a paragraph format?		
	If there are two or more policy statements, did you use the outline format?		
Chapter 8	Did you include a *Definitions* section?		
	Did you define all abbreviations, acronyms, technical terms, jargon, forms, and commonly misunderstood words used anywhere in the policy or procedure?		
	Did you write concise definitions?		
	Did you write summary level definitions?		
	Will the audience understand the definitions?		
	If a term or object is technical, will a non-technical person understand the definition?		
	If an object was defined, did you include a reference statement?		
	If there is an appendix at the end of a policy or procedure, is there a corresponding definition in the *Definitions* section?		
	If you pointed the reader to an external location for a document, is that document easy to find?		
Chapter 9	Did you include the *Responsibilities* section for your policy or procedure?		
	Did you write summary-level statements in the		

	Responsibilities section?			
	Did you write the roles and responsibilities of the *Responsibilities* section in conjunction with the action-type events in the *Procedures* section?			
	Did you write the *Responsibilities* section in an outline format?			
	Did you use the active voice instead of the passive voice?			
	Did you include a compliance statement as the first sentence of your *Responsibilities* section?			
Chapter 10	Did you include a *Procedures* section in your policy or procedure?			
	In the case of a policy document, did you write "Not Applicable" under the *Procedures* section if that section was not required?			
	Did you write the *Procedures* section in an outline format?			
	Did you follow the sequence of events for the *Procedures* section as depicted in the flow chart and task list?			
	Did you verify that the roles and responsibilities of the *Responsibilities* section parallel the events in the *Procedures* section?			

REFERENCES

Bates, Jefferson D., Writing with Precision, Sixth Edition, Acropolis Books LTD, Washington, D.C., 1993.

Page, Stephen B., Achieving 100% Compliance of Policies and Procedures, BookMasters, Inc., Mansfield, Ohio, 2000.

Page, Stephen B., Establishing a System of Policies and Procedures, BookMasters, Inc., Mansfield, Ohio, 1998.

Sorenson, Sharon, Webster's New World Student Writing Handbook, Prentice Hall, New York, New York, 1992.

Part 3

Sample Policies
and Procedures

Procedure (case study)	Ordering "Maintenance, Repair, and Operating" (MRO) Supplies
Procedure	Organization Charts and Announcements
Policy	Bank Accounts

PURPOSE OF SAMPLE POLICIES AND PROCEDURES

Sample policies and procedures have been included for reference purposes. These examples will give a sense of what is acceptable when writing policies and procedures. You are welcome to use the ideas in the documents, although you should decide if they apply to your company's applications and culture.

The following notes refer to the sample policies and procedures:

- The template shown is an example only
- The reference statements (for the objects that are defined) are for example purposes only: The referenced documentation is not actually shown
- The table used in the *Revision History* section in the sample documents has been created with a graphic; the current version of Microsoft Word does not seem to permit tables within tables

		Document No.	1000
		Effective Date	2/14/01
Ordering "Maintenance, Repair, and Operating" (MRO) Supplies		Revision Date	
		Revision No.	1.0
		Page No.	1 of 9
		Approval:	

1.0   Purpose

This procedure establishes guidelines for the business processes by which employees can request the purchase of MRO supply items that have a cost of $500.00 or less and are not-for-resale. The process begins with the initiation of a Purchase Requisition form and ends with the payment of an invoice.

2.0   Revision History

Date	Rev. No.	Change	Ref Section
02/14/01	1.0	New Procedure	Not Applicable

3.0   Persons Affected

All employees authorized to initiate purchase requisitions, purchasing personnel, receiving and accounting clerks, and suppliers

4.0   Policy

The policy of the ABC Company is to ensure:

4.1   All expenditures of company funds for purchases are properly reviewed and approved prior to commitment.

4.2   The Purchasing Department is the only department that is authorized to engage suppliers through Purchase Orders and contracts.

4.3   The Purchasing Department follows published guidelines for obtaining the best "purchase value" for requested supplies.

4.4   Personal items (e.g., flowers, refreshments, personal subscriptions, or gifts) shall not be procured or received by the company through the Receiving Department or anywhere on company property.

4.5   The Purchasing Requisition form is the only document used by employees when requesting MRO supplies from the Purchasing Department.

4.6   The Accounting Department is the only department that pays funds to a supplier in accordance with the duly authorized purchase order.

5.0   Definitions

5.1   Maintenance, Repair, and Operating Supplies (MRO). Expense supplies used by employees to help them perform their jobs. These supplies can include small tools, cleaning supplies, office supplies, and a variety of other consumable items.

5.2   Purchase Requisition (PR). Three-part, pre-numbered, form used to request the purchase of supplies or services by the Purchasing Department. The PR is the key document authorizing the purchasing department to buy specific supplies and supplies. Refer to Appendix A for a sample form and form instructions (not actually shown).

	Document No.	1000
	Effective Date	2/14/01
Ordering "Maintenance, Repair, and	Revision Date	
Operating" (MRO) Supplies	Revision No.	1.0
	Page No.	3 of 9

5.3 <u>Request For Quotation (RFQ)</u>. Three-part, pre-numbered form used by the Purchasing Department to request bids from suppliers. A request for quotation is a means of inviting bids from prospective suppliers. The RFQ is the buyer's first official contact with suppliers. The quality and content of the RFQ can determine the outcome of the bidding process because it sets the stage for discussions and negotiations. Refer to Appendix B for a sample form and form instructions (not actually shown).

5.4 <u>Purchase Order (PO)</u>. Five-part form used by the Purchasing Department to establish a legal contract between the company and a supplier. The PO is written evidence of a contract between the buyer and the supplier for the purchase of supplies and services at an agreed price and delivery date. The issuance of the PO is based on formal or informal bids and proposals. The PO should contain general instructions, standard terms and conditions, space to describe the agreement fully, and the signature of a duly authorized agent for the company. The PO is the only document that can be used in transactions for the purchase of equipment, materials, supplies, and services. Refer to Appendix C for a sample form (not actually shown).

5.5 <u>Receiver</u>. Four-part, colored and collated set of paper used to create a receiving document from an issued PO. The Receiver serves as a proof of delivery and the document that records the inspection, acceptance of goods and services, and payment approval. See Appendix D for a sample form and form instructions (not actually shown).

5.6   <u>Packing Sheet (PS)</u>. A form a supplier uses to accompany the order to the ABC Company. Normally, a PS is two-part, pre-numbered, form issued by a supplier when filling the order. This form should accompany any items being shipped to the company from a supplier. All packing sheets must make reference to an authorized and issued PO number.

6.0   <u>Responsibilities</u>

6.1   The Purchasing Department Executive shall ensure compliance to this procedure.

6.2   Employees are expected to select the most current PR and adhere to the guidelines of this procedure when requesting MRO supplies. Employees should obtain necessary approvals from their management and from the Accounting Department prior to submitting the PR to the Purchasing Department.

6.3   The Purchasing Assistant shall review all incoming PR's to ensure that the PR's are completed in accordance with the current purchasing policies and procedures. The Purchasing Assistant shall coordinate any discrepant PR's with the requesting employee. The Purchasing Assistant forwards all approved PR's to the Purchasing Manager for review and election of a buyer.

6.4   A Purchasing Manager shall review PR's and assign the appropriate buyer.

6.5   The buyer shall review the requisition, select at least three sources (suppliers), solicit bids, review bid packages, select a supplier, issue a PO, and monitor the receipt of the supplies.

6.6   The Receiving Department shall monitor the receipt of the order, inspect the order, report any discrepancies, and process the paperwork to the appropriate departments to ensure timely payment.

6.7   The Accounting Department shall process the receiving documentation and generate the paperwork to authorize payment to the appropriate supplier.

7.0   Procedures

7.1   Establishing Need

7.1.1   Any authorized employee can create a PR to purchase MRO supply items in accordance with the requirements referenced in this procedure. The employee should normally review several catalogues or past department orders to get an estimate of the total order value of the PR. This research will aid the employee and his manager in deciding if the PR is a useful purchase.

7.1.2   The employee will complete the PR and obtain signatures for the estimated value of the order. If the estimated value is lower than the value of the order, the buyer will return the PR. The signature levels are:

Up to $250.00
   Employee
   Supervisor

$251.00 to $500.00
   Employee
   Supervisor
   Manager

7.1.3 Upon receipt of the appropriate approvals, the employee will forward the PR to the Accounting Department for review of the budget, charge number, and authorization signatures. The Accounting Department will return the PR to the requesting employee with an approval decision.

7.1.4 If approved, the employee will remove the last copy of the PR for his records and forward the original PR and a second copy to the Purchasing Department for review and order placement.

7.2 Purchasing Department Activities

7.2.1 A Purchasing Assistant will review all incoming PR's to ensure compliance with this procedure. He will ensure that the signatures are correct and that all fields have been properly completed in accordance with the form instructions attached to this procedure. The Purchasing Assistant will initial the PR's at the bottom right corner and then forward the PR's to a Purchasing Manager for review.

7.2.2 A Purchasing Manager reviews PR's and assigns them to the appropriate buyer responsible for the purchase of MRO supplies. The Manager will initial the PR's next to the initials of the Purchasing Assistant and will also assign a buyer.

7.2.3   The buyer will review the PR and begin the necessary negotiations with selected suppliers to find the most competitive bid.

7.2.3.1 At least three suppliers are selected from published lists, Purchase Order histories, blanket orders, or from new suppliers. Two copies of the RFQ are mailed to each supplier; and the third copy is retained in a buyer's open status file. The buyer should allow two to three weeks for the supplier to return a bid package if the requester's deadline permits adequate bidding time.

7.2.3.2 The buyer reviews the returned bid packages and makes a selection; in some cases, the suppliers will be contacted for further discussions about price and services offered.

7.2.3.3 The buyer then selects the best bidder in accordance with internal purchasing guidelines. The best bidder is not necessarily the bidder with the lowest price.

7.2.4   A PO is awarded to the selected supplier. The original PO and first copy are forwarded to the supplier. Copy 4 is forwarded to the Accounting Department. Copy 5 is forwarded to the Receiving Department.

       7.2.4.1 The supplier should review the order and return the acknowledgement copy to the buyer. Copy 3 is forwarded to the buyer.

       7.2.4.2 The buyer shall review any changes in the terms and conditions before approving the final order.

7.3   <u>Receiving Department Process</u>

7.3.1   Upon receipt of the PO, the Receiving Department shall create a receiving document based on the issued PO by using pre-collated, four-part colored paper. This receiving document is now called a "Receiver."

7.3.2   Upon receipt of the order from the supplier, the Receiving Department compares the material received to the Packing Sheet and Receiver. The receiving information is recorded on the Receiver and any discrepancies are noted. The Receiver is distributed as follows:

       7.3.2.1 Copy 1 is forwarded to the appropriate buyer.

       7.3.2.2 Copies 2 and 3 are forwarded to the Accounting Department.

7.3.2.3 Copy 4 is retained by the Receiving Department for 60 days, after which the file copy is discarded.

7.4   Accounting

7.4.1 The Accounting Department files two copies of the Receiver with the current copy of the PO as received from the Purchasing Department.

7.4.2 Upon receipt of the invoice demanding payment for the order, the Accounting Department will verify that the PO copy, Packing Sheet, and Receiver match before they initiate the process to pay the supplier in accordance with the terms and conditions of the PO.

7.4.3 The payment is sent to the supplier of the order in accordance with the terms and conditions of the Purchase Order. A copy of the check is filed with the original order.

		Document No.	4000
		Effective Date	1/10/01
Organization Charts and		Revision Date	5/10/01
Announcements		Revision No.	1.2
		Page No.	1 of 6
		Approval:	

1.0 Purpose

This procedure establishes guidelines for displaying a departmental structure in a published format, for publishing announcements of organizational changes, and for processing the necessary paperwork simultaneously.

2.0 Revision History

Date	Rev. No.	Change	Ref Section
01/10/01	1.0	New Procedure	Not Applicable
03/16/01	1.1	Stapled set of charts is replaced by a three-ring binder	7.2.5 7.3.2
05/10/01	1.2	Human Resources added as a review signature for all organization charts	6.1.2 7.1.4

3.0 Persons Affected

All employees of the ABC Company.

4.0 Policy

The policy of the ABC Company is to ensure that:

4.1 Organization charts and department announcements are provided in a timely manner to identify and communicate the departmental structures within the ABC Company as they happen.

4.2 Organization charts and department announcements are reviewed and approved by the Human Resources Department.

4.3 Organization charts and department announcements are maintained, coordinated, published, and distributed by the Policy Development Department (a part of the Human Resources Department).

5.0 Definitions

5.1 Organization Chart – Visual illustration of a departmental structure. The chart includes each function name, the incumbent's name responsible for that function, and the assigned title for all management personnel within the department. The chart may also include various professional positions and any function that reports to the cognizant department executive in a "dotted-line" capacity. The chart will normally reflect the current support functions as well (e.g., assistants, support staff, and so on). See Appendix A for a sample of the "Organization Chart" layout (not actually shown).

5.2 Department Announcement – Written confirmation of a change in a department (new person, promotion, restructuring, etc.). The announcement is normally prepared by the cognizant department executive and presented to the Human Resources Department for standardization and publication. A standard presentation format is used and distributed to all management personnel.

5.3   <u>Department</u> – The term "department" represents all functions within the authority of the cognizant department executive (i.e., person who reports to the President of the company and oversees the functions of a specific department).

5.4   <u>Management Bulletin</u> – One page announcement flyer on special letterhead with the words, "Management Bulletin," printed along the top center of the letterhead. See Appendix B for a sample (not actually shown).

6.0   <u>Responsibilities</u>

6.1   The Department Executive (of each department) shall ensure that:

     6.1.1   Accurate and current organization charts are maintained and published for his department.

     6.1.2   The paperwork for employee changes is quickly processed and that a current organization chart and department announcement accompany the paperwork to the Human Resources Department for review and approval, and publication.

     6.1.3   The corrected, or redrawn, organization(s) charts and department announcements are forwarded to Human Resources for review and publication.

6.2   The Compensation & Benefits Manager shall:

     6.2.1   Verify the integrity of organization changes, department announcements, and the necessary paperwork required for changes to a person's personnel record in Human Resources.

6.2.2 Coordinate any corrections with the cognizant department executive.

6.2.3 Coordinate the publication of the organization charts and department announcements with the Policy Development Manager.

6.3 The Policy Development Manager shall standardize the organization charts and department announcements, review and obtain the final signatures, and publish the organization charts and announcements.

6.4 The Office Services and Printing Department shall make copies and distribute both the organization charts and department announcements to the appropriate distribution lists. Department announcements will be published on company authorized bulletin boards.

7.0 Procedures

7.1 General – Preferably, the organization chart and the department announcement will be published simultaneously.

7.1.1 When new people are hired, transferred, or other major changes are being made, a new organization chart is required. For each change, other than title or monetary changes, a department announcement shall accompany the organization chart.

7.1.2   The same comments in 7.1.1 hold true for the announcement. If an announcement is deemed necessary, then there shall be an accompanying organization chart change.

7.1.3   Each time there is a change involving title, addition, deletion, or change in personnel, the following documentation is required:

7.1.3.1 Personnel change forms
7.1.3.2 Organization chart
7.1.3.3 Department announcement

7.1.4   If the above documentation is not complete when received by Compensation & Benefits, it will be returned for reason of being incomplete. Should the documentation be sent to the Policy Development Department, it will be forwarded to the Compensation & Benefits Department for review and evaluation.

7.2   Preparation of Organization Charts

7.2.1   Departments can prepare organization charts in any format for submission purposes. The Policy Development Manager will standardize the charts prior to final review, approval, and publication. The charts will be printed on the "Organization Chart" form referenced in Appendix A (not actually shown).

7.2.2 A revised organization chart shall be published for any change.

7.2.3 The organization charts typically reflect management functions. On occasion, the cognizant department executive may wish to show professional designations and various support individuals.

7.2.4 For every chart, with the exception of the President's first line chart, there will be two approval signatures in addition to a review by the Human Resources Department signifying that the charts have been reviewed for accuracy.

7.2.5 Distributed charts will become a part of the "Organization Chart" manual (3-ring binder).

7.3 Preparation of Departmental Announcements

7.3.1 Departments can prepare department announcements in any format. The Policy Development will standardize the announcements prior to final approval and publication. They will be printed on "Management" bulletin letterhead and distributed to all management. The Office Services and Printing Department will post the bulletin on the major bulletin boards throughout the company.

7.3.2 Distributed announcements will become a part of the "Organization Chart" binder maintained by the Human Resources Department.

Bank Accounts	Document No.	3000
	Effective Date	2/10/00
	Revision Date	3/02/01
	Revision No.	1.1
	Page No.	1 of 3
	Approval:	

1.0 Purpose

This policy establishes guidelines for setting up bank accounts and for establishing an authorized signature list for withdrawals.

2.0 Revision History

Date	Rev. No.	Change	Ref Section
02/10/00	1.0	New Procedure	Not Applicable
03/02/01	1.1	Petty cash withdrawal amount increased from $40.00 to $50.00	6.5

3.0 Departments Affected

Finance Department. All other departments are excluded from withdrawing funds from company bank accounts.

4.0 Policy

The policy of the ABC Company is to establish bank accounts as required for such purposes as payroll, remittance deposits, sight drafts, worker's compensation, and general disbursements.

5.0 Definitions

5.1 Authorized Signature List – A listing of company personnel who are authorized to make withdrawals from company bank accounts for any reason stated in this policy. See Appendix A for the current list of authorized signatures. (Not actually shown)

5.2   <u>Bank Account</u> - A record of financial transactions, e.g., a commercial checking or savings account.

6.0   <u>Responsibilities</u>

6.1   The Finance Department Executive shall ensure compliance to this policy.

6.2   The President and Chief Executive Officer (CEO) shall assist the Finance Department Executive with the verification and approval of those individuals entrusted to withdraw company funds.

6.3   General Accounting shall maintain copies of bank signature cards, ensure sufficient cash is available when needed, and remit all surplus funds to the company's treasury operations department for cash advance repayments or investments.

6.4.   Finance personnel shall be held accountable when entrusted with the authority to withdraw company funds.

6.5   The Petty Cash Custodian shall control all employee requests for cash withdrawals under $50.00. Refer to the "Petty Cash" procedure, No. 3100 maintained by the Human Resources Department. (The procedure is not shown.)

7.0   <u>Procedures</u>

7.1   The establishment of any new bank account, or changes to the authorized signature list, requires the prior approval and assistance from the Finance Department Executive and the President and CEO of the company.

124

	Document No.	3000
	Effective Date	2/10/01
Bank Accounts	Revision Date	3/02/01
	Revision No.	1.1
	Page No.	3 of 3

7.2 Bank accounts for petty cash funds shall not be established as company bank accounts; instead they will be opened in the name of the person assigned as the Petty Cash Custodian at the time the fund is established.

7.3 Actual signatures are required for the "Authorized Signature List" except a facsimile signature may be used in lieu of one manual signature where indicated by an asterisk in the list in Appendix A. The facsimile signature plates are maintained and controlled by the company cashier (General Accounting). The current authorized bank accounts are listed below:

Depository Account: 000-100-200
Bank A, Fictitious City, Anywhere
Authorized Personnel:
    Finance Department Executive
    Controller

Payroll Account: 000-100-300
Bank A, Fictitious City, Anywhere
Authorized Personnel:
    Finance Department Executive
    Controller
    Payroll Manager

Disbursement Account: 000-100-400
Bank A, Fictitious City, Anywhere
Authorized Personnel:
    Finance Department Executive
    Controller

More … Not shown in this example